THE FIRST FIFTY YEARS OF PEACE RESEARCH

The First Fifty Years
of Peace Research
A Survey and Interpretation

DAVID J. DUNN
Keele University, UK

Routledge
Taylor & Francis Group

LONDON AND NEW YORK

First published 2005 by Ashgate Publishing

Reissued 2018 by Routledge
2 Park Square, Milton Park, Abingdon, Oxon OX14 4RN
711 Third Avenue, New York, NY 10017, USA

Routledge is an imprint of the Taylor & Francis Group, an informa business

First issued in paperback 2018

A Library of Congress record exists under LC control number: 2005020614

Notice:
Product or corporate names may be trademarks or registered trademarks, and are used
only for identification and explanation without intent to infringe.

Publisher's Note
The publisher has gone to great lengths to ensure the quality of this reprint but points
out that some imperfections in the original copies may be apparent.

Disclaimer
The publisher has made every effort to trace copyright holders and welcomes
correspondence from those they have been unable to contact.

ISBN 13: 978-0-815-39774-8 (hbk)
ISBN 13: 978-1-138-62097-1 (pbk)
ISBN 13: 978-1-351-14676-0 (ebk)

Contents

Preface and Acknowledgements

This book has been long in the making and too long in the writing.

The making has to do with a career teaching International Relations and Strategic Studies in the course of thirty years and more. It is often said of academics, by those who do not know, that we have a difficult first year or two writing the lectures, and then go on to deliver the same old stuff year after year. Never was this the less so than in the case of International Relations. I had the great good fortune to begin my academic career in a new institution that afforded regular and frequent opportunities for course review and amendment. It was an opportunity that I, and my colleagues, grasped, not for the sake of change, but to make sure that what we did was as relevant as we could make it.

One of my teaching responsibilities over many years was the compulsory undergraduate third-year course on 'Theories of International Behaviour' and subsequent variants thereof. It was usually referred to as the castor oil course: nobody liked it at first, but they were told that it was good for them. And most of them came to the view that it was good: 'it brought it all together' was a frequent verdict. Which was, and is, testimony to the power of ideas. It was in this course context that I was able to incorporate more ideas relating to Peace Research and Peace Thinking and the more I did the more I wanted to do. In part this was down to the introduction to the subject that I got at University College London, specifically John Burton and his colleagues. Despite the dominating influence of Georg Schwarzenberger, we (as students) were not dominated by ideas of power politics. On the contrary, we had an open-ended curriculum, that encompassed behavioural science, animal behaviour, systems thinking, philosophy and the like. Burton's work 'Systems, States, Diplomacy and Rules' (then in draft) was our second-year text. In short, we were never bound by the limits of the conventional wisdom and when we needed to change frameworks, we did so. Ideas were not set in stone or self-evidently relevant.

Ideas exist in context and, especially for students of international relations, a context that was and is always changing. So did the theories and approaches that we sought to encompass – and the events that we sought to explain. My approach was – and still is – that ideas evolve in relation to events, fads, fashions, problems and the unknown. Chronology and incrementalism are therefore fundamental, as is context. My justification for a chapter on context, if one is required, was provided at a spot north of Santa Rosa, California in the summer of 2000. Watching the traffic go by on the freeway, I observed that there were a large numbers of very large automobiles. Whatever happened to the oil-shock of the 1970s, I asked. The answer? The young never knew it and the old choose to forget. My thanks, for that, to Joaquin Espinosa and, to him and Audrey for their hospitality over the years; perspective also changes with place.

I thank, also, those who were in at th e beginning and were sources of inspiration throughout: Michael Banks, John Groom, the late Michael Nicholson, Tony de Reuck and Chris Mitchell. Principally, I want to acknowledge the inspiration of John Burton. He was in at the beginning and has been a constant companion since, even at a great distance. It all began with him at University College in London forty years ago. I owe him a great deal and so, too, does the Peace Research community. It is therefore fitting that this book is dedicated to him.

The writing process took far too long and now I have a reason why this was the case. I began this work in an optimistic frame of mind, determined to show the power of ideas to change things for the better. Things, however, got worse and the recent reversions of conceptions of empire, dominance and the politics of political Realism at th e start of the twenty-first century have been hard to take: in fact, depressing. Nevertheless, I sought comfort in Kenneth Boulding's dictum – 'Don't get it right; write it.' If there is some repetition here, and there on occasion, then I defend it as a means of exhortation in difficult times. The way things are is not the way they have to be. It is ap propriate that I th ank, most sincerely, my editor at Ashgate, Kirstin Howgate, and her several assistants (over the years) for her (and their) patience and faith that this work would see the light of day.

What this work amounts to is an impression of the development of Peace Research as it has seemed to me. At this stage of my career, I think that I can make a virtue of age. This is how it seemed to me over the course of four decades. By way of conclusion I ask the question that I ask of students: so what? What does it all amount to? What has been the journey and what has been the achievement?

When I began my career, systematic research involved card-files and library tickets. Now we have the internet, search-engines and all th e rest. If I stress the earlier years of the enterprise, I make no apology, since I th ink that, from this perspective, it is i mportant to stress o rigins, structures and processes of development, especially when so much of it, in evitably, drifts into memory and forgetfulness. The more recent content is easily accessible. A competent student can access files across the globe in minutes, so my task of choosing the 'x most important articles' and 'the n most important books' in Peace Research seem to be a waste of time and effort. Content Analysis and systematic surveys can yield the answers swiftly. My hope is that this work will stimulate others, especially younger scholars, to have a look and see what Peace Research has to offer.

Finally, in terms of format, but principally in terms of the task, I thank my wife, Gill, for her support and encouragement that made sure that this book reached completion. 'The John book' was for her; this one is for him, with gratitude, from both of us.

Stafford, 2005

Introduction

'The twentieth century was the most murderous in recorded history. The total number of deaths caused by or as sociated with its wars has been estimated at 187m, the equivalent of more than 10% of the world's population in 1913' (Hobsbawm, 2002). Moreover, the experience of total war in living memory has been dramatically presented to us by Michael Burleigh's recent reinterpretation of the Third Reich: in the course of the Second World War, the dead a mount to a daily average of 18,000 for a period of almost six years (Burleigh 2000).

Pondering on those observations might lead us, as human beings, to reassess the way we think about wars in particular and our wider social arrangements more generally, especially since violence seems to be a commonplace, within families, societies, communities and states. And where people are not the victims of crime, they are seemingly frightened that it might come to them. As a consequence of that reassessment we might then move on to restructure our socio-political structures to at least minimize violent conflict. That this has not happened is telling in itself. It is telling insofar as it reveals our tenacious adherence to certain assumptions that are deemed to be, variously, lessons of history, the inescapable condition of humanity, the power of original sin and the like. We are, it is said, imperfect and condemned and conditioned to participate in a consequent struggle. Such is the nature, power and persistence of what we might term the conventional wisdom.

Nowhere has the practical significance of this accumulated wisdom been better summarized than in the words of the American social thinker Robert Nisbet, who argued that 'whether we like it or not, the evidence is clear that for close to three thousand years, down to this very moment, Western civilization has been the single most war-ridden, war-dominated and militaristic civilization in all of human history' (Nisbet 1976 p.21). This verdict, which sets Hobsbawm's focus on the twentieth century into a much longer perspective, may be due in no small part to aspects of the conventional wisdom which inform practical politics and diplomacy. For example, the statement of Vegetius, dating from the Fourth century, arguing 'Let him who desires peace prepare f or war.' Similarly, the notion that 'my enemy's enemy is my friend' or 'there are no perpetual friends or perpetual enemies, only perpetual interests.' To a significant extent PR represents nothing less than a major assault on this kind of thinking. It also starts from the rather radical assumption that if we seek peace, then we should prepare for it. The conventional wisdom may be flawed in its logic, unsound in its practical implications and responsible for many of our problems. It is surely incumbent upon us, for example, to explain to this and future generations why and how it was that something of the order of 50,000 nuclear weapons were deployed as a means to stable peace, but a peace that was based on strategies to incinerate societies, if need be.

Yet not everyone accepted the logic and the implications of this conventional wisdom. A few, audaciously and courageously, took on the accepted wisdom –

about war, conflict and violence – and sought to demonstrate that 'peace' was not some Utopian and unattainable state of being, but something that could be understood anew and that practical consequences could follow from the accumulation of new research about peaceful relationships, in the context of many social systems, domestic and international. In the 1950s a small group of scholars, building on the work of an even smaller number of pioneers, formed the nucleus around which 'Peace Research' was to cohere. How and why they did what they did, and when, and how that small and 'invisible college' survived, grew and prospered, to bec ome a significant intellectual presence fifty years later is the subject of this book.

This book is not a detai led history of Peace Research. My aim is more significant than a detailed survey, for the record, as it w ere. In what follows my principal aim is to show how – a nd why – PR developed as an intellectual endeavour in the course of five decades, a period marked by major transformations in global politics. That the focus was to be on research, the discovery, articulation and practical i mplications of new knowledge was the point. Peace Research was not only about a personal stance, nor political protest: many peace researchers were personally committed individuals and some of them did protest. But the guiding ethic was to be found in a search for knowledge, and then its practical relevance and implications.

That Peace Research has survived and developed in the course of those fifty years is b oth remarkable and significant, not least in light of the forces ranged against it; t he (sometimes acrimonious) debates within and beyond it; an d the dynamic socio-political realm in which it h as sought to be relevant. Stated succinctly, PR was not bound to succeed: many wanted it to fail and when it did succeed they cast doubts about it foundations, agenda and academic validity, as we shall see. That PR has succeeded and that it now prospers (relatively speaking) makes it worthy of both recognition and serious treatment.

Opponents asserted that it was both audacious and unnecessary, seeking to address issues already seriously and properly addressed in extant disciplines and fields of study. Many asserted that what we can know of war and peace we already know. To reiterate a p oint that has had a p rofound effect upon our collective consciousness for centuries, in terms of what may be te rmed the conventional wisdom, the human race was condemned to s truggle with its own intrinsic limitations and many aspects of the human condition were said to be inescapable, capable of amelioration at best. This much we had learned from the accumulated knowledge and wisdom of centuries of study. Thus we turned to established fields of study as founts of this knowledge, such as (military) history, philosophy (Ancient and Modern), international politics. From this established perspective, endeavours such as PR were surely 'Utopian', 'unrealistic' and the like. Others argued, with great conviction, that there was nothing new under the sun.

In the course of addres sing the principal aim, several objectives are addressed as well. To illustrate that the early years of PR were modest and that the circumstances of its development were hardly comfortable are of ten forgotten. Moreover, its d evelopment was not without controversy, from within and from without. In the 1960s there was a significant radical element within PR and in the

1980s critics argued that Peace Studies (much in evidence in Britain at the same time that the Cruise Missile issue dominated much domestic debate) was tendentious. It was at about this time that many of those motivated by protest over Cruise joined in with the peace movement and some moved into PR. Yet, on occasion, it was as if they had joined as a car joins a motorway, looking to the destination, not where the road has come from. In discussing where PR is at fifty, it is important to see how we got there. This is not just a case of history for the sake of completeness either. As we move forward, the past recedes and we summarize what we think we were about then. But it is important that we are accurate in our summaries and it is also important to recognize that for each group that engages with discussions of peace and conflict there is no need to re-invent the wheel. And there is more: we can also engage productively with the conceptual agenda that is represented by fifty years of accumulated research: there is much there that is old, but not dated. There is much that is of value, both practical and heuristic. When we engage with what seems like a new problem, we do not have to start with a blank sheet. Much has been done, even though much remains to be done – as we shall see.

In looking at where PR has come from, we are then able to set some observations into a different context, not least because some recent observations about the nature, and evolution, of PR seem puzzling. Some seem to be at best partial, perhaps, even, sometimes wide of the mark. Most recently, PR in its early years has been characterized as 'defensive' and 'empiricist,' indeed having a 'positivist slant' (Terriff et al 2000 p.6 9). To be sure, when PR was getting established, peace researchers were keenly aware of the need for research:, that it be rigorous, rooted in theory and soundly based epistemological bases; indeed founded on, and acutely aware of, the need for awareness of, evidence and foundations, rather than merely polemical or hortatory. Though there was an element of empiricism (how much war? How much peace? When? Where? Why? How? In what circumstances? Associated with what socio-political structures and processes? All of this seems a sound rationale for data gathering and the search for evidence, but empiricism was neither the dominant nor the guiding goal). Research – conceptual, creative and innovate – was both goal and method. Some were devoted to the empiricist approach, but not all. Hence, peace *research*: which term encompasses creative thinking, critique, comparative analysis, innovation in the handling of conflict and so on. But while much of this is research, it is not out and out empiricism.

Moreover, as discussed below, what is striking about the pioneers of PR was not so much their defensiveness as their sheer audacity: they took on the weight of a cultural-intellectual apparatus supposedly rooted in thousands of years of history. Looking at the careers of Kenneth Boulding, Elise Boulding, David Singer, Johan Galtung and John Burton, there is one word that never, ever springs to mind: they were never defensive. More to the point, they were bold, courageous, and iconoclastic and in so saying that of them it is hardly credible to suggest that PR – to which they had contributed much – could have been in any sense defensive. In point of fact, the early decades of PR were marked by a degree of self-consciousness, an eclecticism in terms of methods and selection of perspectives and an expansive, rather than restricted agenda. It is important that we get it right.

In a similar vein, Martin Shaw, in the context of a longer discussion of war and the military aspects of society, provides a brief resume of peace studies, and makes the point that 'peace studies do not, however, themselves form a coherent intellectual discipline' (Shaw 1991 p.7). Accepting the point that PR and peace studies are not exactly the same (an issue to be discussed shortly), he observes that peace studies is construed as a k ind of 'alternative' Strategic Stu dies or International Relations – an d some may find this a perfectly acceptable construction. Indeed, in the early days of the Stockholm International Peace Research Institute (SIPRI) was regarded by many as a bit 'alternative'. It was not unusual to hear the remark that, though its data and reports were 'alright', it was SIPRI: many preferred the data that came out of the International Institute of Strategic Studies in London: the IISS was after all, authoritative. It was concerned with strategic issues; SIPRI was, well, SIPRI and concerned with 'alternative' things, like peace. Anecdotal, maybe, but not less significant for all that. (And it is worth noting that, these days, SIPRI is quoted as an avowedly authoritative source, without qualification, without reference to any thing alternative or oth erwise. Significant in itself, surely, and no mean achievement).

Yet the question of coherence is significant: PR is indeed coherent, insofar as it is a v aried, eclectic an d open-ended academic enterprise, with the question of war, conflict and peace at its centre. Shaw argues of the peace researchers that 'their sociology seems limited and ad hoc,' which, whatever else it suggests, seems puzzling. Looking back, peace researchers seem to have been remarkably keenly aware of their location, connections and goals. Indeed, as part of the creative and innovative tasks of PR, to be 'ad hoc' might be seen to be a positive strength. Ad hoc does not mean, of course, 'anything goes,' but it is p art of the research task to be creative, innovative and not bound by the existing paradigms, models and approaches. Also puzzling is Shaw's observation that peace studies lacks historical perspective (Shaw 1991 p.7), especially in light of a survey of the emergent issues as PR developed, seemingly keenly aware of t he need to root th e search for alternative approaches in an understanding of how we got to where we were.

If the works of, for example, David Singer were not rooted in the search for an historical perspective on the incidence of war, it would be hard to say what they were about.

Thirdly, Bill McSweeney has recently suggested, like Terriff et al, th at PR can be characterized in large part as p ositivist, but he goes on to suggest that the framework of the Cold War gave PR something to shoot at, a clear targ et, but that 'the sudden end of the Cold War has left the formal organization of Peace Research bereft of a cl ear focus' (McSweeney 1998 p.6). This seems remarkable. Even during the Cold War, the agenda was more diverse, varied and enriched than McSweeney's comment would suggest. At the same time it can be argued that PR has revealed a clear con tinuity of purpose and an expansion of tasks and goals as circumstances have evolved. Moreover, the case can be made – and is here – that the end of the Cold War has thrust the PR agenda more into focus and into the intellectual mainstream, as many look to the world after the demise of Cold War hostility to e xamine the nature of alternative security structures, ethnic conflict, terrorism, 'failed states' and the massive agenda of 'peacekeeping' and 'peacemaking'. What kind of peace can be made and what kind of peace is being kept? It is a major objective of what follows to demonstrate that, in fact, PR has survived only because it has been devoted to a cont inuous process of task expansion in the course of fifty years. Only by adapting has it remained relevant and only by adapting could it have survived. Indeed the case can be made that PR is more relevant now than ever, as we struggle to cope with new questions of security and peace.

What is i ndeed remarkable is th e following comment from Ken Booth, Professor of International Politics at the University of Wales, Aberystwyth: 'the teachers of strategic/security studies during the Cold War rejected as irrelevant (or worse) the work of those "radicals" in peace research or world order studies whose conception of peace and security was far broader than the high politics of mainstream security studies...Prominent among the radicals were Johan Galtung's writings about structural violence, Kenneth Boulding's concept of stable (as opposed to u nstable) peace, John Burton's individualist rather than statist world view and Richard Falk's world order as opposed to realist values'. More to the point, he continues, 'I would argue that their insights constitute a more original set of contributions to the present security debate t han *any* of the articles that have been filling space in the workaday security journals at he closings of the Cold War' (Booth 1997 p.86). This comment ought to be taken seriously. The pioneers were, indeed, marginalized where they were recognized at all. They were, it was asserted, self-evidently unrealistic and not dealing with the issues that were at the centre of the agenda: except that they were, but their stances and positions were not recognized by those with a dif ferent frame of reference. The peace researchers were being realistic in their own terms, but they were not bound by the tenets of Political Realism, the approach that dominated International Relations for much of the twentieth century, and neatly summarized in the oft-quoted aphorism of Hans Morgenthau: 'international politics, like all politics, is a struggle for power.' No qualification, no ifs and no buts. This is, it is asserted, the way it is.

The question of visibility and recognition are still p ertinent, as t wo recent publications demonstrate. Griffiths and O'Callahan survey the key concepts of International Relations and the work is as up-to-date as it can be. (Griffiths and O'Callahan 2002). Y et what is conspicuous is that in this otherwise admirably comprehensive work, there is no explicit entry for 'peace' and nor is there one for 'conflict'. To be f air, there is an entry on 'peace thinking' but not an explicit attention to two key concepts which are, surely, central to our agenda. They are not alone in omitting such discussions.

The 'Fontana Dictionary of Modern Thought' contains an entry on 'Conflict Theory,' which seems to h ave been written despite the fifty years of PR (here defined to subsume the analysis of conflict: we shall see why this is the case as we proceed), not because of it. The entry suggests that 'conflict theory' is a response, in terms of sociological theory – n arrowly defined – t o the limits of Parsonian structural-functional theory, as this related to the dominant approach to social theory decades ago. To be sure, Parsons cast a long shadow over (especially American) sociology in the 1950s and beyond. Equally, such dominance was sure to prompt a 'radical' response' (after all there were major social conflicts in the 'stable' society of the United States of the 1950s, race being not the least of them) in terms of social theory. But 'Conflict Theory' is wider, more sophisticated and richer than this entry even begins to engage – in an authoritative source book – not about social theory (narrowly defined) but 'modern thought'. To repeat, this work would lead us to believe that barely anything had been done in regard to socio-political conflict, save in respect of a narrowly-defined response to the limits of a dominant social theory in a given time and place. If the issue is narrowly defined, then this should be ackn owledged at the outset. If a wider field is to be encompassed, then the task should be followed through in its widest implications. If the approach is narrowly defined without reason or explanation or reason, then we have a major, clear and significant problem. Of commission and omission.

But if 'modern thought' is a n otion to be engaged in its entirety and its modern context, then it should be engaged in all of its contemporary breadth and significance. Old approaches should be recognized, new challenges identified and relevant – an d successful – ch allenges properly acknowledged. This, after all, seems, relevant, reasonable and contemporary, as well as a recognition as to how modern thought evolves and adapts to new circumstances. It is also a responsible stance in relation to a dynamic field not only of social thought but also social conduct.

It is, of course, thought to be rather 'bad form' to criticize authors for what they do not do or say. It is a professional norm that one should address what they do say and say certain things in a certain way. But it is surely incumbent upon us, in difficult times, to ensure that when we search for relevant frames of reference to cope with a difficult world – of Srebrenica as well as New York – that we avail ourselves of *all* of the existing scholarship. We need to be a ware that knowledge changes and evolves. If a partial perspective is to be a dopted, for reasons of neatness or concision, then this is a fair stance, duly acknowledged. But sins of omission surely either ought to be acknowledged and where they are n ot, then identified. It is, as is argued here, too important to miss and – as Boot h tells us – there is more to it than meets the eye, not least the extent to which PR has engaged with realistic issues and concerns, even when they are not Realist.

So visibility is a real problem and one of the objectives here is to pay attention to PR: to make it more visible. But also to offer observations and judgments which need to be set side by side with some of those identified here. Empiricists, defensiveness, lack of coherence, ad hoc, loss of focus do not sit easily with my own understandings – and experience – of PR. I claim no superiority in respect of the perspective presented here, but I do offer a di fferent perspective, based on how it seemed to me then and as it seems to me now.

A survey is also timely. Fifty years is as good an anniversary to celebrate as any other and, undoubtedly, many of the pioneers would have thought getting through fifty years beyond their wildest expectations, if not their hopes. But there is an additional need. Andrew Mack's survey of PR is now dated, with a perspective in the 1980s (Mack 1985) and Pardeesi's survey is even older (Pardeesi 1982).

Being timely, however, is more than merely recognizing the passing of time, important though that is. Survival is worthy of celebration: for PR, even more than normal. But it is a point worth re-iteration: PR is not, and never was, an academic enterprise for its own sake. It was, in its origins, a response to hard times when the survival of the human race on this planet was itself an issue of great moment. It could hardly be said of our own times that we live in a period of peace and tranquility. Enquiries about the idea of peace, its construction, its implementation and its practical consequences can hardly be more timely. We live in hard times: as Tom Paine would have it 'these are the times that try men's souls' – and women's, a significant point in itself: like most other enterprises, PR has recognized questions of gender.

So, by way of orientation and clarification, just what is 'Peace Research'? PR is an intellectual enterprise devoted to answering a simple – or is it a complex – question: what are the causes of war and conflict and what are the conditions of peace? At least that was the defining and orientating question which has been refined to include the questions that relate to the causes and consequences of conflict and violence in all socio-political systems, war being the most visible of these. And, second, what are the manifold implications of and manifestations of the notion of peace, the absence of international wars, specifically the absence of nuclear war, being the most conspicuous manifestation of this idea? How and why these initial definitions and stances came to be widened and invested with more meaning, by way of definitional content and an operational agenda, we shall address in due course since it is part of our remit to address how and why Peace Research took the form that it did in light of its initial defined stance and primary agenda.

Chapter 1

Setting the Context

This chapter seeks to establish a dynamic context within which the evolution and development of Peace Research can be set. Ideas do not simply emerge; they are responses to events and especially moods and changes. This as especially been the case in Peace Research.

The reasons for looking at contexts are clear. To say that Peace Research has sought to be relevant begs the question: relevant to what? To say also that the agenda of Peace Research has been dynamic is also to beg the question, what is the dynamic that drives it? Thirdly, it needs to be established that many who are interested in Peace Research currently have no direct experience of, or memory of, the circumstance in which it developed. Moreover, and as a corollary, it is perhaps necessary to observe that those who may know of events and context may not be aware of, or misunderstand, the interplay of events, and the consequent effects upon the research agenda and research dynamic in peace research. It is no fault to state the apparently obvious connections, for they are often misunderstood.

Peace Research did not develop in a vacuum. It started in one – difficult – set of circumstances and evolved as circumstances changed. But it was not always clear as to how things were changing and why. It is something of a commonplace these days to say that things might have evolved in a different way. But one of our habits is to feel that the way things developed is the only way that they could have developed. But this is not so.

The aim of this chapter, therefore, is to set the scene, as it were, and establish the context within which PR changed. Insofar as a key objective of PR was relevance, it is important to ask, 'relevant to what'?

The Decade of the 1950s

At the start of the 1950s the transition into the Cold War was well underway. The United States was avowedly a superpower, possessing the atomic bomb, and well on the way to the acquisition of the hydrogen bomb. The Soviet Union was also, by now, a nuclear power and, by June of 1950, the first 'Hot War' of the Cold War period had begun, in Korea. Events there were to have far-reaching consequences. Whereas, for example, before Korea, the purposes of the North Atlantic Treaty Organisation were profoundly political, the outbreak of fighting in Korea led to decisions that would see the deployment of four divisions of United States troops in Europe and the establishment of a sophisticated military command structure in the alliance. Korea also changed some attitudes and reinforced others. In Britain, the period of austerity, which came to be a watchword for the period between 1945 and 1951, gave way to an ex pansion of public spending and a peri od of rearmament (not without economic consequences as post-war recovery continued). The attitudes of those who saw the world evolving into a confrontation between capitalism and communism, east against west, good against evil and Christianity versus godless atheism were reinforced. Communism was clearly spreading from Moscow, to China and now to Korea. And onwards to...?

In the United States, the domestic political agenda was dominated not only by the defence requirements of the Cold War bu t also by the mood of a nti-Communism. The intervention in the Second World War gave way to a continuing commitment to the defence of Western Europe and 'The West', but this process was incremental rather than automatic. And even putative allies were not always treated in as friendly a manner as one might have expected. Nuclear cooperation with Britain was abruptly terminated in 1947, the Roosevelt – Churchill agreement signed at Hyde Park notwithstanding. Lend-Lease had been similarly abruptly ended at war's end. The collective mindset changed in response to perceiv ed challenges in Greece (which gave rise to the Truman Doctrine of 1947), the Berlin Blockade and the Czech coup in 1948, the Soviet acquisition of the atomic bomb in 1949 and the success of the Communist Revolution in China later in the same year. Espionage was deemed to be part of the reason for the perceived failures of U S policy that these events were said to represent. The sense of 'loss' that underpinned the response to the success of Mao in China should not be underestimated. Senator Joseph McCarthy and the events associated with the House Un-American Activities Committee came to embody the personification of the American mood of the time.

Yet the War in Korea was indecisive. After a year of movement the war gave way to two years of relative immobility and Truman's popularity plummeted (to be matched by those of Nixon thirty years later in the course of the Watergate saga). Dwight D.Eisenhower, a popu lar soldier in the Second World War, replaced Truman as President and presided over the United States for the rest of the decade. The Fifties was marked by the development of nuclear strategies. At first, for the Americans to have an atomic capability seemed to be policy and strategy enough. A key goal for politicians and military alike was 'more' in answer to the question 'how much is enough'?

The articulated strategy of the 1950s for the United States appeared in 1954 in a speech from Eisenhower's Secretary of State, John Foster Dulles. In January 1950, the Secretary of State, Dean Acheson, had in effect delimited a zone of US influence in the Pacific in a public speech. There was, he suggested, a line through Japan, to Formosa, the Phillipines and to points south which represented a zone of American interest and concern. Korea, it w as suggested, was Stalin's attempt to test the validity of this claim and, with it, American resolve to commit, fight or both in the context of the evolving Cold War. Dulles pointed to the error in the Acheson premise by saying that, in future, the United States would respond massively at times and places of its own choosing: from here on, it would not call the shots ahead of time and say what the United States would or would not do, where or when. Such uncertainty allied to the threat of retaliation would serve to deter any would-be enemy i.e. Stalin's Soviet Union.

Through the rest of the decade the strategy was implemented and the means to implementation developed. Bombers increased in numbers and to these would be added the evolving family of inter-continental ballistic missiles. At first these were large and liquid-fuelled (later th ey became more conspicuous as the American, and a world, public watched the developing space programme and spectacular launches of satellites, then men and women), but technology provided smaller missiles, solid fuelled and capable of being made more secure in underground silos. By 1960, nuclear propulsion of submarines meant that there was an incentive to deploy missiles on these revolutionary submarines, now rendered almost impossible to find at sea and, consequently, rendered invulnerable. Thus, with bombers, missiles and submarine based-missiles, the United States developed the strategic triad, as a means to invulnerability, stability and security.

In due course, the Soviet means followed suit, so that much of the decade and beyond was characterised as an arms race, s o-say with its own self-fuelling momentum. To its proponents it was a means to security and stability. To its opponents it was a cert ain madness, suitably embodied in its description of Mutually Assured Destruction.

Nor was this all. At the end of the Second World War many assumed that the European empires would be re-established after the wartime effort. This proved to be a m onumental delusion. The war had changed many things, not least the relations between the Europeans and their imperial subjects. Japanese victories in the Far East had demonstrated the vulnerability of the Europeans; they were not invincible. The British, French and Dutch found that re-establishment of Imperial authority was easier said than done. (And, parenthetically, it is worthy of note that whatever else article 5 of t he NATO treaty said, it was made clear, de f acto, that the United States would not fight to re-establish European imperial interests: this is why the 'North Atlantic area' was defined as it was). In 1948, British India disappeared; the Raj was no more and its end was bloody in the creation of a new India and a div ided Pakistan (the appearance of a s eparate East Pakistan, as Bangladesh, was still decades into the future and the issue of Kashmir remains on the contemporary agenda).

The French defeat in Indo China in May 1954 was catastrophic. Surrounded at Dien Bien Phu, they were not relieved and were beaten. Which event had key consequences. The Geneva Accords set up new successor states in South East Asia – Cambodia, Laos and two zones of Viet Nam, with elections in these last planned, but never held. After defeat in Indo China, the French resolved to draw the line of Imperial retreat in Algeria, thus heralding a bloody conflict that lasted until 1962, which precipitated much bloodshed in Algeria and in France, as well as massive political instabilities and no little civil commotion (much of it not made public until years later). De Gaulle was called for in a moment of supreme crisis and restored stability with the advent of the Fifth Republic in 1958, even though there were those who wanted him dead and went to great lengths to secure this end.

The British found themselves fighting in Malaya, Kenya and then Cyprus, seeking to resist threats to their re-assertion of authority, and failing conspicuously in the debacle th at was 'Suez': it was a moment, an escapade and a watershed. Colluding with the French and the Israelis, the British sought to o verthrow Nasser in Egypt. A dominant view was that, like Hitler and Mussolini before him, he was a dictator who needed to be removed; if he were not, he would harm British strategic interests in the Middle East, then a zone of British interest, with the Suez Canal a v ital strategic interest for the British in particular. The British failed in their military objectives and withdrew when Eisenhower threatened the stability of the British currency. Yet the affair served to reveal the mismatch between British assumption about what it could – and should – do an d what it was, and was not, capable of. Britain after Su ez was a c hanged state, and a c hanged society was on the way.

As Empires fractionated and fell, 'Europe' became an idea as well as a place and the 'European Project,' for s ix states at a ny rate, was a m eans to econ omic transformation and political significance. After the end of the Second World War, Churchill was firmly of the view that European Union was a wonderful thing – but not for the British. The Europe of the six thus developed to transform the economies – and social systems – of the constituent members A peaceful system of relations was emerging in Europe, where the Westphalian system itself had emerged four hundred years before.

But it was not all about politics. What was also significant was the power of social norms. Women then were, of course, to know their place and be subservient. The marriage vows of the Church of England were clear that women were to obey their husbands. Divorce was, in effect, social disgrace. Society was ordered, stratified and stable and individuals were, consequently, deferential. Women knew their place, in the kitchen. Children were to be seen and not heard. Homosexuality in Britain was illegal and Lesbians invisible. The punishment for major crime was execution: and this was deemed to be the natural order of things. The watchword of social conformity was 'respectability' and the response to problem was 'discipline'. Poverty was still a problem, as was racial discrimination in the United States: but society was stable. Therefore it was good. So many people were, in consequence, rendered minorities: Blacks, women, immigrants and the poor. Murderers were hanged and homosexuals deemed criminals. The rest 'did the right thing.'

But the norms came to be ch allenged. Deference gave way to protes t. Conformity and repression gave way to expression and difference. The end of conscription in Britain allowed, if it did not stimulate, the growing of long hair in males. Many young people came to ask the question 'why'? And, as time went on, the answer 'because' was not en ough. In t he United States, the civil rights movement gathered pace, and with great consequences.

Yet, in retrospect, the decade was a decade of austerity, reconstruction and coming to terms with the effects of the war. To many, it was simply dull. If Auden could say of the Thirties that it was a low, dishonest decade, Norman Mailer said of the Fifties that it was the worst decade kn own to man. Many sought ways of escape.

The Decade of the 1960s

In the United States the shift out of the Fifties and into the Sixties was best exemplified with the election of John F.Kennedy to the presidency in 1961. For Kennedy, the torch had been passed to a n ew generation and nowhere was that generational shift more evident than in the juxtaposition of Dwight and Mamie Eisenhower on the one hand and John and Jackie Kennedy on the other. Ike and Mamie were of another generation, the soldier turned president, now old and infirm. John and Jackie were the coming generation, he the youngest President and she the embodiment of the new style that owed less to the post-war generation and hinted rather more at what was to come.

Domestically, things were changing more substantively too. The emancipation of the slaves pronounced after the Civil War a century before was, only now, coming to fruition with the successes of the Civil Rights Movement. This was not entirely peaceful and some enduring images of that time remain powerful today, intervening images notwithstanding. Soldiers barred the way to Black schoolchildren making their way to school; Black men and women were dragged from lunch counters and humiliated; water cannon was aimed at peaceful protestors, police dogs were set on others. Some Civil Rights activists were murdered. Yet the Civil Rights movement succeeded, in law and then in practice, and the transformation of much of the United States was set in train. Against the forces of conservatism, things could be changed and the way things were was not the way they had to be. The examples set here did not go unnoticed elsewhere.

In Britain, as the fifties came to a clos e, the Conservative Prime Minister, Harold Macmillan, observed that 'we had never had it so good' and for millions this was undoubtedly the case, but it was all relati ve. Many acquired a television set, but it sat i ncongruously in their nineteenth-century built slum homes. The welfare state (part of the post-war Labour Government's 'New Jerusalem'), allied to growing prosperity, saw many in Britain joining in the search for, and involvement in, the consumer society. Jobs were plentiful, safety nets had been put in place by the post-war Labour government, in terms of health provision and social insurance, and key industries had been t aken into public ownership. Standards of housing improved dramatically, in due course, though it is worth commenting that the new housing schemes that saw the end of the old slums were themselves soon to be dee med problem areas and many were demolished within thirty years of their erection. Such was the shortage of job that many people came to Britain from, especially, the West Indies in search of work. British society began to change. In edu cation, the development of a meritocracy was clear to s ee and those children clever enough to pass examinations received state support to allow them to proceed on to university (the numbers of which expanded dramatically by 1970), which would have been impossible for many thousands before 1939. There were the beginnings of social mobility, across class as well as in spatial terms. Yet, at the same time, many thousands of people employed in traditional industries before, during and after the war would see major disruption to their working lives as these traditional industries shrank. Within a f ew years, there would be but remnants of once thriving industries such as te xtiles, shipbuilding and heavy engineering. Many British cities would be transformed in consequence. One explanation for this wholesale transformation was the changes in the world economy. By the advent of the sixties, Japan was the leading shipbuilder (employing new methods compared to those in Britain). Indian, Egyptian and other textile industries threatened, and then replaced, the British.

By the sixties, austerity faded into the past and as the decade proceeded, British foreign and defence policy began to shift. As we have seen, Suez represented a watershed. The 1957 Defence White Paper saw the British strategy shift to a reliance on nuclear weapons and a smaller, professional armed force. Conscription was to be ended by the early sixties. Decolonisation was, by now, well under way. For many British it seemed to be a regular occurrence that a member of the Royal family or government eminence was to be present at the ceremonial handover of power in a myriad of places. There were, consequently, new flags to recognise and new names to learn. Yet, as the decade passed, it became clear that the appearance of decolonisation was more apparent than real. There were new flags and anthems and the like, but the colonial experience was not thrown off as easily as many assumed. To be sure, there was shift in global industry in some degree, but though this did challenge some British and European centres of manufacture, it did not set in train the wholesale transformation of the new state. In the context of the Cold War, those who did not fit into the dominant structures of the Cold War, East and West, inhabited a new political space known as 'The Third World'. As well as degrees of poverty and deprivation, the legacy of colonialism was to be the problem of viable states (academics turned their attention, at this time, to the agenda of 'nation-building'; by the late 1990s, we would be looking at the problems of failed or non-viable states) and ethnic differences that persisted over decades and frequently led to discrimination and violence.

Yet in Europe there was a remarkable optimism. France had been transformed from a peasant economy, in many respects, into an impressive, confident and modern state of great economic strength and consequent political ambition. In the Federal Republic of Germany, the 'German Economic Miracle' was a real achievement and the Germans were transformed; members of NATO after 1954 and strong, confident allies (but, still, with some strings attached). Italy was likewise transformed into a modern, integrated state, even with some persistent regional divisions. These three states, together with Belgium, Netherlands and Luxembourg constituted 'the Six', those members of the European Economic Community who had united together on the path to European integration. By now the benefits of their endeavour were clear to see and the British, after Suez and the realisation that a new agenda was in prospect, turned their attention to membership of the Community. As recently as 1957 they were not at all interested in membership. In 1962, de Gaulle refused to have them as members.

In addition to changes in politics and industry, there were profound social changes in the offing. If the fifties saw the arrival of 'Rock and Roll' in the United States and Europe (and recall that the earliest images of Elvis Presley on television depicted him from the waist upwards, so outrageous was his behaviour then thought to be!), the sixties saw the arrival of Pop Culture. Many saw rock as a disruptive influence, encouraging rebellion and anti-social behaviour. Certainly the conformist decade of the fifties seemed to be receding at a growing speed. Conscription had ended in Britain, which might have had something to do with the fashion for longer hair amongst men, with The Beatles in the van and the even wilder Rolling Stones following. The influence of American culture saw many wanting to partake of it and then add their own cast. By 1964, the pop revolution was well underway and the importance of it as a means of changing society more widely should not be underestimated. Increasingly, the young had more to do, more to spend and more to say. They did not, now, have to do as they were told. Increasingly, a woman's place was not necessarily in the home. Sex was not to be talked about in hushed tones, when it was talked about at all. As the critic George Melly termed it, we had turned 'revolt into style'. And, in turn, Bob Dylan told us that, indeed, 'the times were a changin''. In Britain, for example, homosexuality was de-criminalized, as was abortion (subject to certain criteria) and capital punishment was ended.

Many therefore thought that change was not always for the better. John Kennedy was assassinated in October 1963, a year after the Cuban Missile Crisis that saw the world on the edge of disaster. It was not long before his brother, Robert, was shot dead, as was Martin Luther King, the prominent Civil Rights leader in the United States. And Vietnam crept onto the agenda, then dominated it: for weeks, months and years on end. It gave rise to the massacre at My Lai. The war undermined Lyndon Johnson's plans for the transformation of the United States, to so-called Great Society. It ended Johnson's political career and left him a broken man. It also produced some of the most significant and lasting images of the twentieth century: the self-immolation by fire of a Buddhist monk, the killing of a man by shooting through the head (and the continued filming of his blood running onto the street) and the image of a small girl running from an area hit by napalm. And, in turn, it provoked and then stimulated domestic protests against the war that were followed elsewhere. If the Civil Rights Movement had demonstrated what could be achieved in one realm, it might work in another.

And these were followed by protests about more than the Vietnam War; they were protests about the international order, the domestic order and conflation of much else. It was in these sorts of circumstances that pioneering works that questioned traditional assumptions started to appear and these, in turn, would serve as turnkeys, stimulating enquiry into an agenda that would, it seemed, expand endlessly. Students contested their exclusion from university decision-making processes and resorted to sit-ins, with the London School of Economics most conspicuous among them. A rubicon, of sorts, was crossed in London in 1968 when there was a massive demonstration against the Vietnam war at the American embassy. Police caught unawares there and then quickly learned lessons about what to do the next time.

The classic 1950s sociology of Talcott Parsons, whose work was massively influential, but which was predicated on the assumption of a soundly-based society largely devoid of conflict (since things were handled so as to preserve the stability of the system), now seemed anachronistic; conflict seemed to be ubiquitous; about race, role, class, gender, authority and the rest. The 'peaceful' system that quietly reproduced itself seemed passé.

And the arrival of the contraceptive pill changed the questions of fertility fundamentally (when? why? how many?). The freedom agenda associated with this issue should not be underestimated. Control was now more important than traditional expectations about what women were supposed to do accor ding to traditional norms. These changes stimulated the debate about the role of women in society (This debate con tinues in societies that do n ot conform to t he western, liberal democratic model.) This was no mere issue of chemistry or technology. It stimulated and fed the debate about the role and function of women, men and marriage in modern society. Women, of course, responded, and vehemently. The early feminist authors were represented by Germaine Greer, in Britain, and Betty Freidan and Gloria Stein em in the United States. They constructed the agenda in general terms: those who came later articulated it and expanded it. In other words, those who articulated the agenda of feminism in the 1980s and later did not invent the wheel: the inventors did.

In July 1969 there occurred an event that was much celebrated at the time and which had revolutionary implications. These implications were not recognised as such at the time (how could they be?). When men landed on the moon they, in association with their predecessors who had gone into orbit, they changed not only the idea of a phy sical cosmology but als o a s ocial cosmology. From space, we could now see ourselves for what we were – an d are: a s pinning ball i n space. Now, the perspective was to shift to the global: international relations persisted, but the definition of our condition as global, and fragile, was to have major consequences.

The Decade of the 1970s

For the United States the decade began as the sixties had ended: badly. The continuing war in Vietnam provoked opposition and then violent opposition to the opposition. In May 1970, in protest at the extension of the war into sanctuary area in Cambodia, students took part in protests across the country. In Kent, Ohio, an area not known for its overt student radicalism, students were fired on by the National Guard and several were killed. In New York City, anti-war demonstrators were confronted by angry construction workers and violence ensued.

As the war became more unpopular and dissent and violence became more conspicuous, the United States government faced a clear di lemma: if it could not win in Vietnam and if it was not to admit to losing, how was it to extricate itself from the conflict? Protracted negotiations ensued and, finally, a deal was brokered which saw the United States exit from Vietnam asserting that the outcome was 'Peace With Honour'. To many it was neither and the lasting images from the end of the conflict were less concerned with images of handshakes and diplomatic tables and more to do with people scrambling to get aboard helicopters to be ferried to w aiting American warships, from which the helicopters, once having delivered their human cargo, were tipped into the South China Sea.

By 1974, Richard Nixon had left the presidency in disgrace and on the verge of impeachment, a direct co nsequence of a break- in at offices of the Democratic Party in the Watergate complex in Washington, D.C. Some of his associates were sent to jail: all were disgraced. Lying in politics was now firmly on the agenda. Some may argue that it always had been, but the Nixon presidency undoubtedly gave rise to a pessimism about politics, indeed an overt and widely-shard cynicism. The Kennedy era now seemed a long time ago.

Yet, for many, Nixon's finest hour came just before the storm broke over Watergate. Recall that Nixon had been Eisenhower's Vice President for much of the 1950s, in a Republican Administration. Nixon, with Henry Kissinger, made overtures to the People's Republic of China which had the effect of changing the role of China in world politics. First, Kiss inger went to China secretly and the unofficial contacts were more public in terms of what came to be called 'ping-pong diplomacy', following the sending of a table-tennis team to China. In short order, the People's Republic was admitted to the United Nations and assumed its seat on the Security Council, at the expense of the Republic of China based in Taiwan/Formosa.

In the context of the 'great game of n ations' that underpinned Kissinger's approach to international politics, this overture to China was clearly a move made with the relationship with the Soviet Union in mind. Clearly relations with the USSR had improved, as signified in the signing of the first Treaty on the limitation of Strategic Arms (SALT1) in 1972. The process of arms control was to continue throughout the decade, if somewhat slowly. Gerald Ford, Nix on's successor (and Vice-President) agreed with Leonid Brezhnev at Valdivostok in 1974 that SALT1 was the foundation on which to develop SALT2, which would finally appear in 1979. But, by then, much else had changed.

If SALT was the benign aspect of superpower relations, then the persistent conflict in the Middle Ea st saw the United States and the Soviet Union in a complex relationship of supporting their respective client states and involving themselves, in October 1973, in a nuclear quasi-confrontation. In the context of the early days of th e Yom Kippur War, when there were rumours of a pos sible intervention by Soviet troops into the Middle Eas t, the United States placed its forces on a second-stage nuclear alert, ev idently as a signal of intent to forestall Soviet intervention. Even in the context of progress in nuclear arms control, the United States-Soviet relationship was, still, one of cooperative hostility.

A direct con sequence of the Yom Kippur War was to dem onstrate the downside of interdependence, which, as both a co ncept and phenomenon, had come to the fore throughout the sixties. The downside was vulnerability and this was made manifest when the world's oil producers concerted their activities (through the Organisation of Oil Producing Countries, many of them Arab states) in order to raise the price of crude oil, with the express aim of raising the pressure on Western states in order that th ey, in turn, would pressurize Israel to give up territories it had occupied in the Six Day War of 1967. In this respect OPEC failed conspicuously. But the actions of OPEC were to have profound effects upon the global economy, since billions of dollars were shifted to consumers in the West to producers, whose economies were transformed. And so, in turn, was the Western banking system and, in due course, the size, shape and the mechanics of global debt. For many Americans, the oil shock saw the end of the large cars that appeared in the era of very cheap fuel and the shift to smaller – and Japanese – cars. The global economy was becoming ever more interdependent. But the idea that oil prices could be made vulnerable to such political forces that OPEC represented made many feel uneasy; this was an 'oil shock.' For many Americans, it was a sign of the world coming to America, where they had been accustomed to America making the world.

Europe, at least in the western region, was becoming more integrated. The British Prime Minister, Edward Heath, signed the Treaty of Rome in 1972 and Britain joined the European Economic Community, with others, in 1972, having been frustrated earlier by President de Gaulle. The Europe of 'the Six' was now growing, attracting the attention of others states and proceeding a progressively more integrated pathway. This was significant in itself but also a symptom of the process of restructuring of global politics consequent on the end of empire. Colonial, then Commonwealth, ties were to give way to an increased commitment to Europe. There were also significant influences on the structure of the defence establishment after the end of empire and the need for 'global reach' gave way to the emergent agenda of working with allies and friends in the European and Atlantic areas. Europe as a place was also giving rise to the idea of 'Europe' as a vision and a goal of integration.

The last significant European presence in Africa disappeared with the fall of the Salazar regime in Portugal. A direct consequence of this was the end of colonial rule in Angola and Mozambique, but the consequences were far from benign. In line with its avowed intention to assist movements of national liberation, the intervention of the Soviet Union into southern Africa prompted a counter-response on the part of the United States. Cold War logic demanded it, for in no circumstances was the Soviet Union to be permitted a cost-free intervention or interference. What long-term aims preoccupied the United States was far from clear, but the Soviet Union was not to be allowed a free run in Africa.

The United States aim in Chile was indeed clear, even it the actions were overt. Salvador Allende had been elected President of Chile. He was a socialist and, thus, deemed to be a problem at best and a threat at worst to the US interests in South America, a traditionally US sphere of interests. The Allende regime was toppled in a violent coup in 1974 and Allende was killed. His regime was replaced. Cold War logic demanded it.

In the context of both Superpower and European relations, much of the early part of the decade gave rise to a mood of optimism. The SALT agreements were both a symptom and cause of this, but the wider context should not be forgotten. The German Chancellor, Willy Brandt, was instrumental. As a former Mayor of West Berlin he clearly was aware of how to manage the politics of tension, but as the Chancellor of the Federal Republic he moved the debate – and the history of Germany – along significantly. His key innovation was to move Germany into the future and free it of its difficult past. Symbolically, and significantly, he kneeled before a war memorial in Poland and apologised for previous events. The watchword was to be 'Ostpolitik' – changing the relationship between Germany and its neighbours to th e east. Boundaries were recognised, the past was acknowledged and now was the time to move on.

In the wider realm, the watchword was 'détente'. Meaning an easing of tensions, the idea of détente was both encouraging and troublesome. In a pos itive sense, it signified a sense of improving relations between East and West that might even be dated from the Cuban Missile Crisis of 1962, when the Superpowers faced each – and learned a lot about the nature of risk. Relations did improve in the early 1970s, epitomised in the Helsinki agreements of 1975, when – in the widest sense – Europe and North America came together to agree a wide agenda of cooperation. But the problem was that there was no rulebook that gave a h int as to how the game of détente was to be played. It was imprecise and gave way to uncertainties.

Especially significant was the question of human rights as embodied in what was known as 'basket three' of the Helsinki accords. The Soviet Union agreed to abide by the questions specified in that agreement and, in consequence, groups of intellectuals and others organised themselves, in the Soviet Union and Eastern Europe, to monitor compliance. These groups were harassed, monitored, imprisoned and treated badly. Nor was this all: the question of Jewish emigration from the Soviet Union to Israel was an issue that became, progressively, a wedge between East and West. The response of the Soviet authorities was that this was an unwarranted interference in the domestic affairs of the Soviet Union and that the United States should attend to its own domestic agenda first.

If this was one example of Soviet attitudes and behaviour, others, it was said, could be found easily. The signing of arms control agreements was one thing. But there was, for many Americans, the question of compliance. It began as an issue in the 1970s and became more significant in the 1980s. And Soviet interventions in Africa and meddling in the Middle East gave many cause for doubt or suspicion.

When Nixon left the White House, his Vice P resident, Gerald Ford, succeeded him. In 1977 Ford gave way to Jimmy Carter. Carter had to deal with a complicated agenda, but above all he had to deal with the post-Vietnam syndrome and a key issue on his domestic agenda was how to reconstruct the United States and restore the public confidence in its leaders and institutions. To some significant degree Carter succeeded. Yet he failed to be re-elected. The inability to free the Americans held captive in Iran in 1979 had much to do with this, but so did the challenge personified in the Republican candidate, Ronald Reagan.

And, as if to s et the seal on th e decade of t he 1970s, with arms control apparently so promising, détente a watchword and European integration proceeding, the decade en ded with the Soviet intervention into Afghanistan. The stage was now set and the agenda clear. But what the meaning of this action was, and what implications that followed from it, were far from clear.

The Decade of the 1980s

In Britain, Margaret Thatcher became Prime Minister in 1979. She did s o with a mission allied to zeal. She sought to free Britain from the shackles of the state and the influence of he trade unions, yet she came to preside over a period of domestic conflict, European opposition to th e policies of NATO and the challenge of military conflict overseas.

In 1977 the German Chancellor, Helmudt Schmidt, had – in a speech to the International Institute of Strategic Studies in London – made a plea for a symbol of continued American commitment to W estern Europe. European concerns, and especially German concerns, centred around the idea th at, in light of increased superpower cooperation arms control, the United States might be less disposed to commits itself to th e defence of Western Europe. The added concern was made clear in relation to the deployment, by the Soviet Union, of new SS-20 missiles, to replace older SS4 an d SS5 ty pes. These new missiles, the deployment of which was perfectly permissible, since they were beyond the remit of the SALT treaties, were deemed to be a *de facto* threat to Western Europe. In what circumstances, such as these, would the United States commit itself to t he defence of Europe? That, in effect, was the question addressed by Schmidt. That he was asking the question as a German only added to weight to its importance. The response was the so-called NATO Dual Track Decision of 1979.

In the autumn of 1979 the NA TO allies agreed to do t wo things simultaneously. On the one hand it was decided to engage the Soviet Union in negotiations to address the questions relating to intermediate nuclear forces in Europe, principally the Soviet SS-20 and, on the western side, Cruise missiles and Pershing II. If the negotiations proved to be unsuccessful, in a period of four years, then the western systems would be depl oyed in Europe. Yet the effects of these decisions and the preparations consequent upon them were to lead to tu rmoil in Europe. Some coalition governments in Europe were rocked as d ecisions were contemplated as to whether or n ot the American systems were to be accepte d for deployment. Public opinion was significantly mobilised and the British Campaign for Nuclear Disarmament, which had been relatively moribund after attracting much attention in the early 1960s, saw a col ossal increase in membership. Across Europe a n ew organisation was founded to concert opinion, the campaign for European Nuclear Disarmament.

Nor was protest solely confined to Europe. In the United States there was the rise of the so-called 'Freeze Movement'. Many had become disillusioned as the nuclear arsenals in both West and East continued to grow, arms control agreements notwithstanding. Indeed, many began to feel that arms control was somehow running out of steam, failing to ach ieve its declared aim s. However, though SALT1, especially, set limits up to which both sides could build, and technically constituted arms control since both sides had agreed to e xplicit treaty restraints, there was fundamental question relating to the credibility of the arms control process. Indeed, these years of 'nuclear concern' spawned a debate abou t the foundations of nuclear deterrence, and drew many responses from philosophers, clerics and, indeed, former military men who questioned its morality. Deterrence was now, for many, part of the fundamental problem.

The debates found wider public concern and articulation with the production of books and films that depicted nuclear attacks (in Britain 'Threads' depicted a nuclear attack on Sheffield (and the film 'The War Game', made twenty years earlier but deemed so shocking that it never was broadcast to a wide audience, came back to pro minence) and, in t he United States 'The Day After' was concerned with a s trike in the Mid West. The mood of anger and mistrust was hardly helped, at least in Britain, with the publication of a government pamphlet telling citizens what they could do in the event of a nuclear attack. Some of the advice was risible and the wider response to it was one of incredulity, entitled 'Protect and Survive' the pamphlet stimulated the stance, personified by the Left-wing historian E.P. Thompson to 'protest and survive'. Many joined him in doing so. Peace politics was high on the public agenda and conflict over the future of Europe and the wider world conspicuous.

With the arrival of Ronald Reagan in the White House in 1981, the 'Second Cold War' was not long in following on. Indeed, with Reagan in the White House, Thatcher in Downing Street and Helmut Kohl as Chancellor of the Federal Republic of Germany, there was now a triu mvirate of the Right in key western capitals, all with a very clear view as to the nature of the Soviet problem: they invaded Afghanistan, locked up dissidents, deployed dangerous weapons, refused to negotiate seriously about the intermediate systems in Europe and assisted regimes in eastern Europe (principally that of General Jaruzelski in Poland, trying to handle the problems associated with the rise of the Solidarity Movement) to repress democratic change. All of this was summed up in Reagan's characterization of the Soviet Union as 'the evil empire'. Reagan, consequently, supervised a massive expansion of the United States defence budget: the Navy, by way of example, was to have no fewer than 600 front-line warships, to cope with the global reach of the expanded Soviet navy.

And then, in 1983, R eagan introduced the idea of a space-based system of defending against a potential Soviet attack on the United States. Given the success of the film that dominated much of the early 1980s, the project came to be known as 'Star Wars'. It was a prospect that, from a Soviet perspective, would have in effect disarmed the Soviet Union, rendering useless all of the weaponry acquired at great cost, economic and otherwise, over decades. Yet, at the same time that Reagan was redrawing the battle lines of the New Cold War, it was also quite clear that the war in Vietnam had had a lasting effect on the likely support of the United States public for the use of military force. Large, overt acts of intervention were to be avoided and when several hundred Americans were killed in Lebanon, when a lorry loaded with explosives was driven into th eir barracks, the Americans withdrew from the region, Reagan's bold rh etoric notwithstanding. Where force was used, in Panama and Grenada, it was limited in pursuit of very limited objectives. But there was still a co ncern about insurgency in Latin America, a traditional American area o f both concern and intervention, as well as with Iran. The two conjoined in t he context of the so-called 'Iran-Contra' scandal, where underhand dealings, clearly too sensitive to be publicly paraded, embarrassed the Reagan presidency. Lying in politics – again.

If there was pessimism and concern in much of Europe and North America, many shared it beyond the regions as the problems associated with global debt became manifest. In fact, the problem of Third World Debt was systemic, related to the dynamics of the global economy as interdependence increased (globalisation was a term that would come later) and the consequences of the massive transfer of wealth from oil consumers to producers were recognised. Great sums of money found their way into the banking system in the mid-seventies and were loaned out to a host of states. Yet i n the short to medium term the ability to repay became more of a con cern. Many states had turned away from food production and transferred to cash crops: when the prices of these fell, or harvest damaged a crop, then many states were caught in a double bind: they had no money and no food. With the debt is sue came increasing concerns about famine and mass poverty. Political instabilities, ethnic differences and corruption hardly helped.

And now there was a key issue of transparency as the images of want and devastation appeared on television screens around the world. Just as the 1960s was associated with the tele-visual consequences of Vietnam, so much of the 1980s was about the images of dead and dying – men, women and children. And, then, there was AIDS.

As if these were not concerns enough, there was also the question of the environment, previously the preserve of the geographers. Long taken for granted, the long-term health of the planet became a p olitical issue, within states and between international actors. Nor was this simply a q uestion of things getting worse and worse. Many of the issues that were addressed by the pioneer writers and activists in the 1960s were now issues of wider concern, debate and response. The Feminist Movement was widespread and the agenda of political and socio-economic choice began to change in consequence. There were now new rights that went with work, maternity leave, employment law and so on. The conformist and deferential social norms of decades earlier were now challenged. The environment was now to be part of this concern not only about rights but also about obligations, to those on the planet and those yet unborn. Traditionally waste had been buried, dumped at sea, incinerated or neglected. These were, in the context of a new system of values, no longer acceptable solutions. The political agenda was becoming 'greener' and in the Federal Republic of Germany the Green Party was hardly inconsequential. We now had to face up to issues of consequence. What did we do with fuels taken out of nuclear reactors? What did we do with the decommissioned nuclear submarines that had been revolutionary and cutting edge technology when they first appeared? What about depleted fish stocks and the toxic consequences of both wars and intensive agricultural methods? Thirty years previously these had been the concerns of pioneers such as Rachel Carson in the United States: now mainstream political parties, in the western liberal democracies at any rate, could hardly afford to ignore them. The Greens were instrumental in making it obligatory for mainstream political parties to engage with environmental issues.

Set side-by-side with this, however, were the first manifestations of the onset of a sort of g lobal culture. Clothing, footwear and the like were now no longer anonymous: they were branded and were became more brand conscious. Those producing these items were doing so from a global production system for a global consumer market. This would be consequential in terms of the shifting of production from high-wage areas to areas of cheaper production, with all that was implied in terms of unemployment in some areas an d new employment opportunities in others. This was not entirely new since changes such as these in sectors such as steel, shipbuilding and textiles had already had important effects, but the new scale of the global shift in patterns of production and consumption were unprecedented. Here too, there were questions about the rights of workers and obligations upon employers. 'Sweated Labour' and 'Child Workers' appeared on the agenda. But so, too, did the rights of non-combatants in undeclared wars, many involving child soldiers. Old rules, it seemed, were not for new times.

However, in terms of the relations between East and West, whose rules of interaction had often seen them intervening in proxy wars in the Third World, things were to change remarkably. The 'Old Guard' in the Soviet Union left the scene: the death of Brezhnev was rapidly followed by the death of his elderly successors, Andropov and Chernenko. The new Soviet leader was Gorbachev, with a mission to be pragmatic and reformist. Gorbachev realised that the very future of the Soviet Union was at stake. As an economy it could produce the *materiel* required to compete with the United States in the realms of defence and space. It was infinitely less capable at producing those goods and services that would make Soviet Man and Woman happier, fitter and more comfortable. It is worth noting that in the last months of the Soviet Union, coal-miners went on strike – for more soap! A major consequence of the new approach from Gorbachev was his enthusiasm to engage the United States in new arms control agreements, the successful conclusion of which would allow a re-ordering of priorities domestically: arms competition could be closed off to some degree and resources diverted into a domestic agenda. The watchwords were to be 'glasnost' and 'perestroika' – openness and re-structuring. The aim was an increased legitimacy in the Soviet system and what he termed 'new thinking' in terms of international security, informed evidently by the evolving debate in Europe regarding a new agenda of 'common security' as discussed by the Palme Commission, headed by the former Swedish Prime Minister.

The first manifestation of Gorbachev's new thinking came at the summit meeting with Reagan at Rejkjavik in October 1986. In a little over three years, the Berlin Wall came down and soon after the Soviet Union and the Warsaw Pact. This was a remarkably short space of time within which momentous events occurred. It was a period not without risk, anxiety and violence.

Nevertheless, the Cold War was over.

The Decade of the 1990s

The end of the Cold War gave rise to a new agenda and no little confusion. Indeed, the analogy that comes to mind is that associated with the decision to halt a supertanker: giving effect to that follows on some time after the decision to stop is made. Moreover, it is no exaggeration to say that many – in government, defence and the academy – were unsure of what to do after the end of the Cold War, so entrenched were the assumptions and patterns of thought – and habits of both mind and bureaucracy. George H.W. Bush soon trumpeted the transition to a New World Order. Fukuyama told us that we had reached the end of history (Fukuyama 1992).

Yet soon we saw the advent of low-tech genocide in Africa where hundreds of thousands were killed: not by atomic weapons, nor by accident, but hacked to death with machetes and clubs. The world discovered Rwanda, Hutus and Tutsis. And Grozhny and Chechnya, the one a city destroyed and the other a place in the former Soviet Union that was largely unknown beyond it. And then Bosnia and Sarajevo, places and names that immediately led on – and back – to considerations on the causes of the First World War, Gavrilo Princip and Archduke Franz Ferdinand.

They were now invested with new and more immediate meanings, and consequences, as 'ethnic cleansing' found a place in the lexicon of the 1990s and where these events were thought to be taking place 'on the edge of Europe'. People were killed for what they were, less than who they were and Yugoslavia disintegrated, not simply under the weight of Bal kan history ('going back thousands of year into history, where East and West met, and with difficulties') but at the behest of politicians with a different agenda, of manipulation of difference and the fostering of conflict. In due course, we would be led to Srebrenicia, where something of the order of 7,000 men and boys were slaughtered (more then double the numbers of those killed on September 11th 2001) as soldiers wearing the blue berets of the United Nations seemed powerless to assist.

In Ireland the 'peace process' was set in motion, agreements were reached and the process of 'delivery' was addressed. Yet, in Ireland, Omagh was bombed and scores killed. In England, the centre of Manchester was devastated by a bomb and the centre of the city was de facto reconstructed in its wake.

Economic security was also on the agenda, with the successive collapse of sectors of the global economy in the course of the decade. In turn Mexico, the Asia-Pacific region, Russia and Brazil were in crisis and – since the process that preoccupied so many was 'globalization' – the ramifications were widely felt. Manufacturing industry was necessarily restructured and not only in line with globalization. The structural adjustment of defence industries with the transition out of the old Cold War environment gave rise to exits from the industry, massive mergers (within and beyond frontiers) and 'downsizing' of the workforce. More widely, in the global economy, companies produced globally for a global market and the issue of identity and culture found their way onto the agenda. Was 'globalization' another word for 'Americanization' and a continuing process of cultural domination – as sociated with baseball caps, McDonalds and the like. In due course, Joseph Nye was to characterize this as an aspect of American power, but 'soft power.' (Nye2004).

As the new millennium approached, major economic summits of the G7 (and Russia) turned into battlegrounds where 'Anti-capitalist' protestors confronted heavily-armed police, most notably, though not only, in Seattle.

The widening economic divide in the global economy, with the rich getting richer and the poor becoming very poor, allied to the transparency of poor living standards in the area formerly referred to as 'Eastern Europe' (when it was part of the Soviet zone of hegemony) but now known as 'Central Europe' by many, led to the process of migration, legal or otherwise. People drifted across seas and oceans, tried to get through fences, tunnels and controls, stowed away in ships and containers, even in the wheelbays of aircraft. And, in due course, 'immigration' became a mainstream political agenda issue in the advanced and developed states. They were others, sometimes illegal and therefore, for many, a problem and even a threat.

'Europe' was increasingly transformed from an idea and then a stated goal of 'ever closer union' to the 'European Union' with a single currency (though not accepted by all) and an agenda of closer cooperation in the areas of defence and security, perhaps even a single European army. The long-dormant Western European Union (revived in the 1980s) became ever-more relevant to developing discussions about the burden of defence that should be borne by the Europeans, and where, when, why and how they could and/or should act independently of the United States. The events of Kosovo were, for many, indicative of the strains developing not only within Europe but also across the Atlantic. And the North Atlantic Treaty Organization (NATO) was affected by these circumstances. Who would have thought, from the perspective of a decade earlier, that MiGs would take their place in the German Air Force alongside American-built aircraft? Or that former members of the Warsaw Treaty Organization would join the NATO Alliance?

These were, indeed, interesting and especially challenging times. They put pressure on institutions, structures and processes and they represented fundamental challenges to ideas, assumptions and standard operating procedures therein. Not least of these considerations was the importance of gender in the armed forces and, indeed, the very notion of what service personnel were to do in the new environment. The rights of women, lesbians and homosexual men in the armed services became an important issue. So too, associated with the new tasks of peacekeeping and strict rules of engagement, it was being asked what service personnel should be trained and equipped to do as tasks evolved in the new geo-strategic environment. In certain areas of the globe (as evidenced by ethnic conflict and the advent of 'warlords) states were collapsing. Thus there was a developing role of protection as well as offensive operations and a de facto duty of care as well as tasks much longer-established.

Nor was this all. At the start of the decade the fighting in Kuwait and Iraq saw the deployment of massive numbers of tanks and aircraft, as well as ships that were capable of affecting events on land from the sea. Throughout the decade of the 1990s the electronics and computer revolution had profound effects on the capabilities of armies, the single soldier and everything in between, such that the discourse was cast in terms of the new Revolution in Military Affairs. Armed forces had different things to do. So too did ordinary citizens as they seemed to be subject to the forces of globalization and the challenges of economic security. Perhaps some people ceased to worry about the threat of nuclear war as the overwhelming security problem, but more and more seemed pre-occupied with threats that seemed more pressing and more immediate: to self, family, job, place and society. Security seemed much more difficult to handle. Society at home was changing and crime (and fear of it) a clear threat to very many. For many, society seemed to have attained a peace of sorts, but it brought with it allied symptoms of fear, alienation, loneliness and insecurity, even death.

Security was now more complex: it never was simple and we would be wise to eschew the notion of a golden age. At the same time we would be foolish to underestimate the power of the politics of nostalgia (allied to 'difference?). So, too, was the agenda of peace more complex. And now it was not a question simply of domestic order within states and the absence of war between states. It was altogether more complicated, a conflation of local and global, the familiar and the foreign (real or imagined). The events in New York and Washington, D.C. in the Autumn of 2001 serve as a graphic and tragic example of that complex of issues. A frontier was there crossed, both literally and metaphorically. Regrettably, the definition of the situation was inappropriate since it was not a case of 'good against evil' and it was surely not a case of 'if you are not with us you are against us.' The situation was much more complex.

Nevertheless, metaphors of war were consistently employed and there was clearly a sense that 'something had to be done'. In the Autumn of 2002, the United States promulgated its new National Security Strategy, with military force a principal element of it. The United States was now the single superpower and, as such, in a difficult world, it was to 'do the right thing' because, in the tradition of American exceptionalism, it was, without doubt, a force for good in a bad world.

Iraq was invaded in the Spring of 2003, the regime of Saddam Hussein was rapidly removed and that the mission was duly accomplished was proclaimed and not without a certain theatricality. Subsequent events clearly reveal the limitations of the assumptions that underpinned the Bush-led strategy in Iraq. On the face of it there seemed to be a poor understanding of the nature of peace: limited conception of the transition to a new political system; manifestly a lack of understanding of any potential resistance; and (Vietnam notwithstanding) clear lack of an exit strategy and any sense of timetable to underpin events. By the late summer and autumn of 2003, American soldiers were being killed daily, hotels hosting major decision-makers were attacked, Italian *carabinieri* in Iraq to cope with the transition to a civil society were killed in a suicide attack, as well as Japanese and Spanish nationals being killed in what appeared to be systematic attacks. Neverthless, in public statements at any rate, faith in realpolitik seemed to proceed undiminished.

Such a complex situation demands and necessitates a more fully considered approach, rooted a different understanding of the questions of war, peace and conflict. It is tempting to suggest that we have a paucity of performance, a lack of appropriate leadership and, perhaps most fundamentally, a crisis of thought.

With the context thus set and the persistence of problems acknowledged, it is to the task of understanding and assessing Peace Research that we now turn. That Peace Research has reached fifty years is interesting and noteworthy. But what does it have to offer by way of an alternative frame of reference? That is a key question to which we must return in due course.

Chapter 2

International Relations:
The First Attempt at Peace Thinking?

War and conflict have been persistent features of the human condition. Some deem them inescapable. Yet what is also inescapable is that the set of assumptions and the assumptions that underpin International Relations and, more recently, Strategic Studies are struggling to cope with the problems of a rapidly changing and seemingly ever-more complicated world. For Mark Hoffman, writing of the situation which obtained two decades ago, 'there is no longer any clear sense of what the discipline is about, what its core con cepts are, what its methodology should be, what central issues and questions it should be addres sing' (Hoffman 1987 p.231. It would be hard to conclude that the situation has improved since. In which case, the crisis of International Relations, for it is s urely in the middle of a crisis of existence, throws into sharp relief th e problems that beset it, b ut also throw into sharp relief the alternative concepts, categories, modes of discourse and research agendas of not only Peace Research but also, for example, Feminism, Cultural Studies and Media S tudies. Like Peace Research before them these later academic innovations have frequently been belittled and marginalized.

International Relations and Strategic Studies are re latively modern innovations. Preceding them were the millions or words dedicated to the human condition in general and aspects of war, peace and conflict in particular emanating from the long Western intellectual tradition, the significance of which has already been highlighted by Robert Nisbet. From the Greeks, Romans and the mélange of the Judaeo-Christian tradition h ave come a series of observations, 'eternal truths' and maxims that have informed centuries of discussion and practical politics and statecraft. There are cou ntless treatises, dissertations and textbooks that embody, interpret and summarize much of this thinking and it would be but duplication to try to summarize it h ere. Yet sev eral salient points are worthy of mention since they are pertinent in terms of what follows.

Thus, war has been deemed necessary, inevitable, a test of being noble even, in light of prevailing circumstances. It h as been part of the inescapable aspect of being human. For Macchiavelli in Renaissance Italy, the problem for the prince was the obtaining and management of power, to his own purpose where family politcs were, by definition, about avarice and lack of scruple.

As recently as the mid-seventeenth century Thomas Hobbes of Malmesbury famously wrote in 'Leviathan' that in the absence of a strong authority to ex ert a degree of order, then there would be 'a war of all a gainst all' and, in consequence, the lives of men and women would be 'nasty, brutish and short.'

At the time that Hobbes was writing, the issue of order and authority were central to developing debate. The Civil War in England saw the king separated from his head and authority shift to Parliament. In the rest of Europe, the Thirty Years War had raged on, associated with widespread butchery, the deaths of millions and the disappearance of much of the infrastructure of 'civilized' life. A response to this, and conventionally signifying the initiation of the western states system, were the several agreements collectively termed 'The Treaty of Westphalia' dating from 1648. The Treaty established the central elements of a system aimed at order where there existed potential for disorder and chaos, and where these were real problems rather than potential difficulties. Significantly, there was to be no authority higher than the state. Authority and power were to reside in the constituent units of the system, the states, large and small. All were to be regarded as sovereign and equal, this last being a fiction, but a necessary fiction that allowed some degree of pragmatic development, rather than an endless debate about relative rights. Following on from these two propositions came a corollary: if all states were to be regarded as sovereign and equal, then there was an attendant rule of non-intervention in the affairs of others. In practice, this has been transgressed often, but no states have sought to invalidate it as a guiding principle of state practice: generally, they have sought mitigating circumstances or humanitarian issues to justify their actions.

What is significant here is that those gathered at Westphalia in 1648 did not outlaw war. Despite the preceding three decades, war still had a legitimate role in the affairs of state and it it was a role that was thought to be reasonable, necessary and defensible. At about the same time the Dutch scholar sought to codify something called international law that would guide leaders and make clear what was and what was not allowable behaviour in the developing 'international society.' There were to be laws of war and wars that pertained to what actions were allowable in war. Custom, practice and convention were important in establishing this frame of reference.

But war was not outlawed. In due course it came to be accepted that this international system of states existed as a special kind of political system, quite unlike domestic political systems. There was no central authority, so there was no pyramid of authority. There was no central source of law, no central source of recourse where fault had been identified. States existed in a sel-help system. It was, in the words of Hedley Bull (Bull 1977) and 'anarchical society.'

Yet the circumstances and the context within which this system was to operate were in a state of flux, accelerated by developments between 1760 and 1820. Here, the synergies associated with three revolutions, perhaps even four, served to accelerate change and, with the general changes, the transformation of war. The American War of Independence, led by several gentlemen slave-owners, challenged the power of Europe and broke away. The Industrial Revolution established a new order or domestic relations, starting in England, and changed the very foundations of power and wealth and, with them, social, political and economic relations. The agricultural system gave way to a system of manufactures, urban centers of power and, critically, mass society. In France, absolutism and kingship were overturned and a new order of society was proclaimed. And there was a rev olution of ideas: in these changing circumstances of rapid an d self-reinforcing change, what was the nature of society, authority, rights, duties, obligations and the like?

This period was a prelude to an accelerati ng process of i ntellectual development neatly summed up by saying that the nineteenth century can appropriately be ter med the century of isms: capitalism, socialism, industrialism, communism, liberalism, anarchism and the rest.

In 1914, all of these came together with telling effect. The First World War began with an event in the Balkans and cascaded into mass – indeed enthusiastic – mobilization. By way of illustration Roland Leighton, on joining the British army, wrote to his fiancée, Vera Brittain (later renowned as a major Radical and Pacifist, directly in consequence of the war), 'I feel, however, that I am meant to take some active part in this war. It is to me a v ery fascinating thing – something, if often horrible, yet very ennobling and very beautiful, something whose elemental reality raises it above the reach of all cold th eorizing.' (Bishop and Bostridge 1998 p.38). Leighton was killed, as was Brittain's brother. By the end of the war millions were dead, cemeteries abounded around much of Europe and, in due course, the Menin Gate at the Belgian town of Ypres would record the names of 54,896 persons killed but whose bodies were never found. The war that was to be 'over by Christmas' ended over four years later. The controversies that surround the nature of the First World War continue, seemingly unabated, to this day.

There were many responses to this but, for our purpose, two are i mportant. Firstly, the League of Nations was established to order the behaviour of states. The United States President Woodrow Wilson (incidentally, a f ormer professor of politics at Princeton University) who greatly pushed the idea of the League, sought to import more openness into interstate diplomacy, making the practices of states more transparent on the assumption that secret deals and interlocking alliances had much to do with the cascade into war in the weeks after the assassination of Franz Ferdinand in Sarajevo. Transparency was allied to a wish to avoid the problem of war by making diplomacy not only more transparent but also more rational. Time was important and so was the opportunity for clear minds and rational thinking to be brought to bear. It may seem quaint from our contemporary perspective, but it is noteworthy that the Covenant of the League made provision such that states contemplating the use of force should giver several weeks notice of their intention to do so. The presumption was that, given time, good offices and common sense would prevail, making force unnecessary. Note, however, that the League, just as did their predecessors in 1648, did not outlaw war, the previous years of devastation notwithstanding. States so ught to be the arbiters of their own destiny. As it is conventionally put, the issues that were never resolved in the peacemaking after 1919 were the tensions associated with improvements in the system sought by Wilson, consistent, with a set of guiding principles or ideals, and the self-interest of states. There lay the classic tensions between the 'Idealism' of the reformers and the 'Realism' of the states, especially the victors.

And here, too, is the duality, or irony, of the question of war and force. It is at once a symptom that order in the system of states has broken down, that peaceful diplomacy has failed, and at the same time, the resort to force is deemed to be a means to establish or res tore order, or resist threats to established order t hat emanate from revisionist or revolutionary states. The League never sought to abolish war.

A second response to the war was to accelerate a mood associated not only with the issue of 'how did this happen?' but how can it b e prevented in future? Clearly, much had been written in preceding centuries about war, order and justice, within the confines of established fields of endeavour such as philosophy, law, history, ethics and the like. But in the view of many what was required was explicit and visible attention to questions of improved diplomacy, knowledge about the international system and averting, if possible, future war, within the principles adhered to by states.

This gave rise to the appearance of International Relations as a d iscrete academic discipline. There were extant organizations before 1914, principally the Carnegie Endowment for International Peace, based in the United States, and the World Peace Foundation. In light of events, more effort was deemed necessary.

Thus, the first Department of International Politics was established at t he University of Wales at Aberystwyth, with the assistance of the Welsh coalowner, David Davies. A department followed at Oxford University as well as the London School of Economics and Political Science and the Royal Institute of International Affairs was established in London at Ch atham House. In North America, the Council on Foreign Relations was established in New York and university departments soon followed (most conspicuous amongst them within a few years was that at the rapidly developing University of Chicago, from which university came Charles Merriam, Harold Lasswell and Quincy Wright). In due course, from these early institutional initiatives came further growth and International Politics came to be taught in universities across the western world (though there were fierce contests regarding the autonomy of International Relations, with critics arguing that it was but a s ub-field of Political Science, rather than a d iscrete discipline; indeed initiatives aimed at making International Relations more systematic and scientific in the 1960s were partly informed by the rather astringent criticism that International Relations was little better than informed journalism).

What were the core as sumptions and goals of this new International Relations? First, it was concerned with the world of states, for the predominant units of political behaviour in the international realm. There were relatively few of them and the major amongst them were responsible for the conduct of good government in the colonies and order in their own states. All the states were deemed equal and sovereign and, as a general rule, were to accept the idea of non-intervention in the domestic affairs of each other. This being the case, the central issue to be c onfronted – as with that confronted by Macchiavelli and Hobbes and their predecessors – was the question of order, in a self-help system with no central authority but with a body of 'international law' which may be disregarded at will, if political imperatives deemed so.

Second, the aim was to improve the quality of knowledge that underpinned the performance of governments, especially given the potential for disorder and where disorder might lead to war, manifestly becoming more destructive in mass societies, where rapid dev elopments in technologic change were cumulative in their consequences. Nevertheless, even though we can discern the elements of we came later to call the elements of the International Relations problematique here (essentially, what was the subject about?), namely order in a system of states, and a paradigm-in-effect, different approaches – that could equally be tolerated or consistent with the elements of the problematique. On the one hand were the rationalist/optimists, who assumed that right reason, law and knowledge could, and would, lead to improved performance in international relations. On the other hand were those who took a contrary view, claiming that whilst the rationalists were being 'Utopian' they themselves were Realists, dealing with the world as it was, not as some might wish it to be. From these two approaches followed different emphases, but they were agreed that they dealt with a world of states. This was the paradigm, this was the shared set of assumptions that united them despite differences, this was what was being researched and taught: this was what International Relations was about.

Questions of methodology seemed self-evident. The presence of order constituted a peace of sorts, but a peace nevertheless, however minimal. This was the problem at the centre, with eclecticism a key feature of the discipline (see Wright 1955 for a survey of what he called 'root disciplines).

However, as these institutional and academic endeavours picked up pace, so did events alter the environment. It was not merely a question of the absence of the United States, Germany and the Soviet Union from the League. Beyond this, military establishments were trying to come to terms with not only the implications of the war (for which many of them seemed so poorly prepared) but also the innovation consequent upon it. Pioneers sought to get to grips with the emergence of airpower, poison gas which could debilitate and not necessarily kill an enemy, and the armoured fighting vehicle, the tank, capable of marrying together armour and the revolutionary speed of twenty miles per hour. Amongst the pioneers of the tank might be mentioned J.F.C. Fuller and Basil Liddell Hart in Britain and Charles de Gaulle in France. With regard to developing the role of airpower, Hugh Trenchard in Britain, Giulio Douhet in Italy and Billy Mitchell in the United States merit serious attention.

The emergent novelties were often resisted, but by 1939 (and after the bombing of Guernica in the Spanish Civil War) aerial bombing of cities, factories and homes was deemed a legitimate objective in war. The major states devoted massive amounts of resources to airpower. But the Second World War aimed to rout Fascism by any and all means. Total war demanded total commitment, total effort and at the conclusion of the war, total surrender. This is not the place to retell the history of the Second World War. But two observations are pertinent.

Firstly, the war saw a further collapse of the limitations on war established in such international society as did exist. Second, given the nature of the war as it developed, the advent of the atomic bomb seemed like a logical development of massed air attacks on societies. The difference was that one bomb from one aircraft replaced thousand bomber raids. At war's end another round of diplomacy sought to improve the performance of the system of states, this time embodied in the United Nations. And, just as with the League before it, the states members of the organization retained the right to use force and make war as they saw fit. The attendant task of the academic disciplines of International Relations (as the subject came increasingly to be labeled, apparently with a wider remit than International Politics, as that term had conventionally been used) and International Law, was to try to improve the conduct of diplomacy through concerted study and effort, devoted to the question or international order, harmony and enhanced respect for law and justice.

International Relations developed rapidly after 1945, especially in the United States and its community of scholars, and its publishing houses, have assumed positions of dominance. With the advent the Cold War, a tract for the times seemed a pressing requirement and one was found: Hans Morgenthau's 'Politics Among Nations' (Morgenthau 1949). There, encapsulated within its covers was not a theory of international relations but THE theory. It was tract for its times and dominated the field for decades. It seemed relevant to the inter-war period (during which Morgenthau left Germany for the United States) and it now seemed entirely appropriate to the new circumstances. What mattered, for Morgenthau, was power; power politics was the essential concern. As if to validate Morgenthau's frame of reference, all we needed to do was to look out of the window: this was the way of the world.

But the world was changing and so was International Relations. Methodological concerns were more explicitly addressed. How did we get to know what we know? Why and how has economics been taken so seriously in the conduct of governments, when International Relations is dismissed as commentary or worse? These were impulses that gave rise to methodological dynamism in the 1960s, as International Relations got to be more 'scientific' – as did the emergent Peace Research, where, in general terms, scientific meant looking at the methods of the natural science, involving data accumulation, theory testing and construction and the like. From this perspective, Morgenthau's treatment of the reality of international relations, though deemed adequate and appropriate by many, began to look imprecise, elastic in its use of concepts and lacking in rigour. However, the optimism of the 1960s gave way to a sense of pessimism allied to confusion. War and economic sensitivities gave rise to newer emphases of economic interdependence and vulnerability. Integration studies gave way to questions of the power of multinational companies and other new 'actors'. To cut a long story short: essentially, in order to take account of these novelties and problems, International Relations has struggled with the question not of states alone at the centre, but 'states plus what?' There is a dynamic at the core of international relations and a focus on states is necessary, but not sufficient. We have thus struggled for more than three decades to find out what elements are necessary and sufficient, whilst also trying to assess the utility of the conceptual maps and categories of discourse that we seek to employ in seeking explanations. In the era of post-modernism, words are not neutral and perspectives are contested. This is the crisis at the heart of International Relations. In fact, in terms of peace, International Relations is now revealed to be a meta-problematique, where a focus on states is revealed as a second-order issue: a focus on human behaviour is required.

Change was now the watchword. Yet the advent of the nuclear bomb had changed things, even though not all immediately recognized that it had done so.

Prescient before the rest was Bernard Brodie, long a student of seapower, who recognized, when many thought that US possession of the bomb was strategy enough, that the role of military power had changed, with a new emphasis of the nature of deterrence, especially once the Soviet Union acquired a nuclear device and a situation of mutuality obtained. The key issue now was what to do with these new weapons in an age of 'superpowers' and where the United States was the archetypal 'national security state.'

Traditionally, 'strategy' is defined as the art of generalship: it is what military men and women do and what cadets study, be it Nelson at the Nile, Eisenhower in Europe or Montgomery in North Africa. Into the decade of the 1950s, however, a new breed of strategists developed; often civilians, many of them working in university departments and research institutes, they were not concerned with the conduct of battles per se, but with the nature of military power and especially nuclear weapons in the new 'strategic environment.' As Alistair Buchan, founding Director of the (International) Institute for Strategic Studies, based in London, effectively defined what he and his colleagues had been doing, he suggested that central to their purpose were 'the political and social implications of the existence of military power, and especially to the conditions for its restraint, reduction and control' (Buchan 1974 p.4). Presumably he would not have ruled out the abolition of war, but nor did he make explicit mention of it as a goal of strategic studies, presumably on the grounds that, as an objective, it was unlikely, unrealistic and perhaps impossible. In essence, strategic studies is about management of weapons, to effective political purposes and with the minimum of risk, given the potential for nuclear disaster in an era of weapons of mass destruction (which ideas comes in linear descent from mass society and total war).

Thus, in due course, strategic studies came to be taught not only in Defence Departments (the old ideas of War Ministries having been consigned to former, and different, times), Staff Colleges and manuals, but also to undergraduates and research students around the globe, encompassing a lexicon to assist in the understanding of international security in difficult times. So, the lexicon expanded: as problems appeared, ways had to be found in order to understand and manage them. There was no existing manual that would do, so ideas of limited wars, escalation, bargaining,, crisis diplomacy, battlefield- and theatre-nuclear weapons, extended deterrence, guerrilla warfare and the like were studied and the policy agenda was informed. Thus, in its modern guise, strategy is clearly policy-orientated, relevant to emergent concerns and political novelties. It has also engaged with a curious vocabulary, a focus of criticism for opponents, but perhaps (psychologically at any rate) necessary for its proponents who deal (or have dealt) with concepts such as 'surgical strikes,' 'collateral damage,' and the like. Yet the abolition of war has been in some respects a peripheral concern, even where it has been addressed at all within the remit of the strategic studies community, guided by the notion that they have to deal with the issues that confront them in real space and real time.

What judgments emerge have sometimes been controversial and some have been alarming. Consider, for example, the following comment from the mid-1950s: 'We cannot simply make the avoidance of both war and communist hegemony an absolute policy requirement…If the choice is put in these narrow terms, the answer has to be th at the United States must prevent the world-wide establishment of communism – even at the cost of total war' (Roberts 1956 p.80). Needless to say, many found this line or arg ument dangerous, a false dichotomy, alarming and a stimulus in the search for an alternative route to world peace. Moreover, this rather alarmist dichotomy – an d the frame of reference out of which it appeared – was hardly passé with passing of decades and the end of the Cold War. In the 1970s and 1980s, an agenda of nuclear use emerged, consistent with the technological development of smaller nuclear warheads. Being smaller, proponents of nuclear use suggested that the yields of these weapons would be sm aller than large concentrations of conventional explosive and that their use would not necessarily preface a rapid es calation to all- out nuclear war. Opponents, especially those in Europe – who assumed that a limited nuclear battle would be more likely to take place in Europe rather than in the Great Plains of the United States – were greatly alarmed at the emergence of this new nuclear agenda. Progress was not necessarily for the better and many deemed smaller to be more dangerous. For their opponents, the proponents of nu clear use were labeled the 'Nuclear Use Theorists'. The resultant acronym seemed rather more accurate and to the point: NUTs.

By the mid-eighties, no less an authority then Lawrence Freedman, an eminent British defence intellectual, came to the conclusion that nuclear strategy was fundamentally in crisis, with, seemingly, no obvious future (Freedman 198). This followed a series of rem arkable initiatives, seriously proposed, funded and tested in the united States to find an appropriate basing mode for the new MX mobile missile. Various options were discussed, declared not possible or viable and abandoned (e.g. Dense Pack, the so-called shellgame alternative and putting missiles on sleds in underground trenches). In due course, fifty MX missiles (now named 'Peacekeeper' by the Reagan Administration) were deployed in existing silos, earlier dee med prone to pre- emptive attacks by the Soviet Union, to which the MX development (as a m obile system) was a response! All of this seemed to raise fundamental question not only about the costs of such systems but also about their credibility.

In pursuit of the avoidance of nuclear war, perhaps even the achievement of a 'nuclear peace' strategies were developed in the course of the Cold War that saw the proliferation of nuclear weapons, to a t otal of about 50,000, with all of the attendant risks of war by accident or miscalculation. And where, in practice, limited wars found a key role.

With the end of the Cold War it might be assumed that this would pass into history. Quite the contrary, for the issue of nuclear use was back on the agenda as the new millennium gave rise to new problems. The agenda of 'global terrorism' (which was hardly a n ovelty on the agenda of global security) assumed new dimensions, specifically within the United States, after the ev ents of September 2001. Consequently, the Bush Administration increased the defence budget massively to fund the so-called 'War on terrorism' and a role was found for nuclear weapons. They were to be developed as a means to penetrate underground control centres, thought to h ouse key decision-makers waging war against the United States, and consistent with the New National Security Strategy proclaimed by the

President in the Fall of 2002. Critics saw this as a dangerous and backward step. Stephen Schwarz, publisher of the Bulletin of Atomic Scientists, described it as a 'nuclear revival' whilst Senator Diane Feinstein saw it as 'a wrong direction and in my view will cause America to be placed in greater jeopardy in the future.' William Arkin, a defence specialist in the United States saw an ulterior motive, suggesting that this was 'a thoughtless strategy being pursued under cover of the war on terrorism by the people who always wanted to do this.' (Quotes from The Weekend Australian, Editor Section December 13-14 2003 p.2).

The point of these remarks is to illuminate the persistence of old habits of thought in new circumstances. They demonstrate that some states are choosing routes to their own security that may even make them less secure, entailing counterproductive policies, allied to the view that, in a period of globalization, where the frontiers of states are porous, 'homeland security' looks rather anachronistic. Moreover, strategies of global security are relegated to secondary status. The logic of Westphalia evidently lives on.

What is Peace Research?

Peace Research begin fifty years ago as a novel approach to the questions of the causes of war and the conditions of peace. It has evolved with changing context and now be summarized effectively, from the ethos of the University of Bradford School of Peace Studies, as attempt to 'analyze the origins and nature of conflict within and between societies and the efforts to build peaceful and equitable forms of social and peaceful coexistence' (Unesco 2000 p.182).

It was therefore a response to the limited ontologies and objectives of International Relations and the often bizarre and dangerous outcomes emanating from Strategic Studies, where threat manipulation was deemed legitimate in pursuit of certain goals. As recently as 1984 Rob Walker could observe that 'contemporary discourse about world politics is still grounded in the specific interests and experience of particularly historically and geographically limited societies, not to mention classes in those societies' (Walker 1984 p.2). Moreover, argues Walker, 'the bottom line of international politics is order, not justice or progress' (Walker 1984 p.10).

This should not surprise us for, from Westphalia onwards, the dichotomy facing decision-makers has been posited as that between order on the one hand and chaos on the other. Faced with that choice, order is preferable. But this then leads, almost axiomatically, to a fear of change or an assumption that political change is a problem rather than a consequent effect of wider cultural, social or technological changes. The problem is clearly posited as how we manage the system to the end of order. This means defining a means of management; but this is often transmuted into an agenda of control and, at worst, repression. We do not have to look far to see how this has been implemented in both international and domestic contexts.

But what kind of thinking underpinned these extant field? Much money was spent and effort expended as part of a search for order in the complex system. Yet many were little concerned with rigorous approaches to methodology. They got on with the job of doing what was required, given what the field was about and their personal interests. Located within a paradigm, they got on with solving what Kuhn came to call 'puzzle solving' (Kuhn 1962). This was what Kuhn called 'normal science' where was an established groundwork, no need to justify terms, where a common language could be assumed and where a set of journals seemed to reflect and justify what was being done. For International Relations and Strategic Studies, the state-centric system assumption was a paradigm-in-effect.

The problem is that we now have a search for a paradigm, of which the confusion referred to by Hoffman is but a symptom. In fact, there is no inter-paradigm debate. There is evidence a proliferation of approaches and explanatory schemes. The proliferation of journals is symptomatic of responses to the crisis of thought. Too many problems are being thrown up, one way or the other, for them to be capable of being relegated to the tasks of 'normal science and research.' Rather, these are problems of a fundamental, even revolutionary, nature. The old paradigm is inadequate, the new is yet to be born.

Whilst some adhere to the old, novelties have emerged in International Relations and the cluster of these novelties constitutes a de facto overlap or convergence with Peace Research. There is, of course, an agenda of change in International Relations, usually labeled 'normative International Relations', of which Cochran (1999) is a good recent example. Most recently, the agenda of Critical Security Studies, involving, amongst others, Rob Walker, Ken Booth, David Campbell, David Mutimer, James Der Derian, Michael Dillon, Jim George and Michael Shapiro. Preceding them we might cite the work of Richard Falk, Saul Mendlovitz and Samuel Kim, at the core of the World Order Models Project (WOMP). This is identified at this stage, to be addressed later.

For Kenneth Boulding, much of this existing 'knowledge' that constituted what it was that we 'knew' was at the root of the problem and, as a pioneer of Peace Research, he not only acknowledged the problem, he also set out towards a solution. Boulding drew a tripartite distinction with regard to knowledge (Kerman 1974). First, he suggests, we develop folk knowledge, that which we pick up along the way; perhaps how to fish, how to win or how to get our own way. This, in turn, accumulates into what Boulding calls literary knowledge: it is that knowledge which is distilled, put into fields scholarship, via books, and reproduced through the practices of education and cultural reproduction. Most of what we know about international politics, war and peace falls into this category, according to Boulding. We have looked at history, used the workings of brain and intellect and surmised about the human condition, that which is eternal and inescapable and that which is mutable. Over decades, centuries and millennia, we come to know what we know, are sure as to what is real and enduring (as opposed to ideal or novel) and define the limits of the possible. Therein lies the origin of the split between Realists and Idealists.

Boulding argues that we need a new kind of knowledge, scientific knowledge, that is grounded not in faith and reason but in methodology, testing, research and rigorous analysis, self-consciously explicated and open to disproof in light of evidence. Science is a procedure, both open-ended and self-correcting. It is a collective enterprise and important for being so (see Bronowski 1978 and Kuhn

1962). But, it might be asked, what is the problem with what we think we know already? Surely, Morgenthau, as a Jew in thirties Germany and who, as a boy, was spat upon, was right to come to the conclusions he did about the nature of human beings and the nature of human nature? He was not wrong to take the view he did as an individual. But the problem lies in the universalisation of this experience as an expression of the experience of being human in general. We cannot fault Morgenthau for coming to s ome of his own personal conclusions. But we can criticize the process of making these observations cardinal elements of his 'theory of politics' and the validity of his inferences. Why did he come to the conclusion that 'international politics, like all p olitics, is ab out a str uggle for power?. Why could he find no significant place for cooperation?

Yet Morgenthau is but one example. Kant, we are led to believ e, was meticulous in his daily routines, almost predictable to the minute in his walks around the town. Yet he spent most of his like in Konigsberg. How was it, therefore, that he could come up with such certainties about the nature of reason, universals and the rest on the basis of such limited life experiences? How could Macchiavelli know how other leaders might deploy their skills in environments that were not Mediaeval Italy? How could he have such confidence that the axioms of political leadership in uncertain circumstances could be so generalizable? And why do we still read him today? Indeed, why do so many in International Relations go back to t he classics of political philosophy? Is it i n search of solace or instruction for a di fficult world – i n 2004 and beyond? And why was it – apart from the problems of unifying a dis parate Germany into a Germ an state – did Hegel come to the conclusion that the state was the be-all and end-all of political organization?

All of this is literary knowledge. It is the canon, having stood the test of time and constituting that which we know about ourselves. But we might do well to be skeptical – perh aps even rejectionist. As we shall see in what follows, Peace Research is fundamentally rejectionist, amongst other things. Peace Research rejects the weight and significance of much that passes for knowledge in the Western intellectual tradition; it rej ects the state-centric problematique of International Relations (as a m eta-problematique) and it rej ects the fundamental assumptions that underpin Strategic Studies, concerned as it is not with the elimination of threats of violence and war, but with their political utility in times if insecurity and uncertainty. The goals of Peace Research are the causes of war conflict and violence, the nature of peaceful human systems and the means of their attainment and the peaceful resolution of conflicts, not necessarily their disappearance. The stance here is n ot to follow the traditional path of research within a given set of assumptions (or a paradigm) following Kuhn (Kuhn 1962).

The fundamental aim is one of re-search, to eff ect a step shift in our assumptions about what is and what is possible. In this it is rejectionist, revolutionary, problem-solving and innovative. This involves a search for evidence, new conceptual schemes and indeed linguistic innovation to facilitate new thinking about human behaviour. The stance that Peace Research strikes against is eloquently illustrated by Mary Clark. Of her students, she said 'they really believed that human history was being inexorably driven by a s et of biologically grounded, rather nasty behavioural traits. Their belief was grounded in the whole Western worldview that they had been immersed in since birth. History focused on powerful men constantly engaged in violent struggles with each other. It never mentioned peaceful societies, nor the lives of women' (Clark 2002 p.xvi).

The very clear presumption was – and still is, by and large – that people are taught what is important and significant, as assumed and verified by authorities old and new. But this also masks the inherent danger that novelties are red uced to categories that we can already know, that our experience is tantamount to all of human experience, that how we feel and go about things is generalizable into a 'theory of human nature' – a condition, moreover, which is deemed not only to be, but to be inescapable. How could Thomas Hobbes know that, if left to themselves, the lives of men and women would be 'nasty, brutish and short'? In the context of the English Civil War, perhaps he was right to be cautious or pessimistic. But what of other times and places?

Is what we have become through centuries of development, war and cooperation still readily reducible to th e essentials distilled from the Ancient Greeks onwards? We might more profitably conclude that what is important is engaging with new ways of thinking, such as Peace Research, rather than constantly re-investigating 'the classics' for inspiration or guiding principles. Progress has been manifest in many areas of human endeavour. That we have made so little p rogress – and continue to pursue wrong policies based on wrong assumptions – in area of socio-economic and political realms may be testimony to our being unwilling or unable to escape from old assumptions in an era o f rapid change. Novel thinking is the key. However, 'normal science, the activity in which most scientists inevitably spend almost all th eir time, is p redicated on the assumption that the scientific community knows what the world is lik e. Much of the success of the enterprise derives from the community's willingness to defend that assumption, if necessarily at considerable cost' (Kuhn 1962 p.5). Forget for a moment the strict definitions about science or n on-science: the assumptions of state-centricity have been paradigmatic in effect, agenda forming and constituting the curriculum. Even though we are phy sicists or as tronomers, Kuhn held up a mirror to us nonetheless, in which we readily see ourselves. Yet what is startling, fifty years after the appearance of Peace Research and the appearance of millions of words, is that so many works, now appearing frequently, to address the issues of peace and security have signally failed to engage with the works of, for example, John Burton, Johan Galtung, Richard Falk and Kenneth Boulding. It is pertinent to include a re mark from Ken Booth: of these four individuals he argues that they were regarded as irrelevant or worse during the Cold War but that their work 'constitutes a more original contribution to the present security debate than any of the articles that have been filling space in the workaday security journals at t he closings of the Cold War' (Booth 1997 p.86).

Mary Clark is, again, perspicacious in her assessment of the problem when she suggests that 'In science, Darwin's phrase "survival of the fittest" was turned into a biological war of all a gainst all, an idea made concrete by the invention of the concept of the "selfish gene". Psychology and Political Science, both obedient to Enlightenment philosophy, mistook emotions as unf ortunate left-over animal traits in need of being tightly controlled by stern paternalistic Reason' (Clark 2002 p.xvi). This is not to discard the importance of the Enlightenment and the exercise of right reason in the development of our collective knowledge. It is, however, important to acknowledge that certain types of knowledge can take us only so far.

A Word on what Peace Research is Not

In suggesting that Peace Research is a new approach to thinking about the problem of war, it is i mportant to establish that there are other stances taken in relation to war, peace an d conflict that are important, but are n ot covered by the rubric of Peace Research.

Peace may be associated with a particular individual or collective life-stance. Here, people make choices consistent with their beliefs about good, bad, harm and injury, benevolence to other human beings and other creatures, as well as the environment. These are well-known. They are respected by some and treated as alternative 'types' by others, perhaps the majority. They are often referred to as 'the usual suspects', prone to tree-hugging, chanting of mantras and the like. As Orwell was once reputed to have described a part of the British Labour Party in the 1930s, they are the contemporary 'quacks, fruit-juice drinkers and sandal-wearers'. They are tolerated as   part of the diverse modern society, but arguably seldom respected.

Likewise, peace protes tors are recognized, but seldom accorded significant status in major debates (though that might be changing in light of the protests that took place i n the prelude to the Anglo-American invasion of Iraq in 2003: th e largest demonstration ever to take place in Britain involved upwards of one million people on February 15 2003). Protest has a long history, but has become even more conspicuous in the last few decades, principally in light of protests against nuclear weapons (the Campaign for Nuclear Disarmament (CND) in Great Britain, the Freeze movement in the United States and the European Nuclear Disarmament (END) movement in many European countries in the 1980s, as well as the protest by women at the Greenham Common air base in England. Before this there were, of course, many and widespread demonstrations against the American war in South East Asia, which were hugely consequential in terms of the war's conclusion. Moreover, the post-war mood in the United States was significant in changing the collective mood, within which Peace Research was defined to be m ore legitimate and less peripheral to political debate.

Religious stances are also important in terms of defining a personal stance in relation to war and peace. Quakerism and Buddhism spring readily to mind in this context. Not all religion s are so clearly defined as these in relation to the central issues and the religious influences in relation to question of the justiciability of war and the question of personal responsibility in war are sig nificant aspects of theological (and sociological) thought. Being a Qu aker or a Buddhist is n ot a necessary or sufficient condition for being associated with Peace Research, but it is a vital connection for some, as we shall see.

This is not the place for an extended disquisition on the nature of religion or the nature and function of political protest. But it is important to recognize that political authorities are wont or prone to dismiss protestors as irritants, suspect in their motives and means employed and tolerated at best. Whether or not they are taken seriously is an issue in need of further research. What is clear is that many protests were dismissed by state authorities as 'politically inspired' or tendentious, subversive and irresponsible. Individuals who led protests were also treated with suspicion by the authorities, the English historian turned peace activist Edward Thompson most conspicuous amongst them.

In order to be taken seriously, in order to be not easily dismissed as the usual suspects and irritants, the pioneers of Peace Research opted for a route to change through knowledge, on the grounds that if good, sound, reputable work could be done, in accordance with the rules of good scholarship, the rules of scientific procedure and collective criticism, then it would be hard – if not impossible – to dismiss as simple alternative thinking, easily dismissable – and usually dismissed. Exhortation and persistent pleas for change would not be en ough. What was necessary was a body of new thought, evidence and information addressed to the problem of war. As Kenneth Boulding put it 'a great deal of the psychological impetus for the Peace Research enterprise came from somewhat dissatisfied members of the peace movement who happened to be social scientists and who perhaps felt that whilst the peace movement provided a very legitimate demand, it did not provide much of a supply' (Boulding 1984 p.1 37 Stable Peace). The demands of epistemological thoroughness (which need not always follow the examples of the natural scientists), new ontological foundations and rigorous methodologies (not all e mpiricist, but necessarily encompassing the search for evidence and consistency) would be key elements in the new venture and it would entail nothing less than the confrontation of the new with the accumulated wisdom of millennia. 'Moral concern and skilful rhetoric will not suffice. But if we can couple our concern with competence and our rhetoric with knowledge, we may yet turn away from disaster. All too many peace researchers and peace activists do not understand that the most important revolution we can make is an epistemological revolution' (Singer 1976b p.10).

Knowledge was the key. Innovation was the aim. Conflict and war were the problems; not to be managed or tolerated (on the grounds that we are doing the best we can in difficult circumstances or we are in a fundamentally inescapable condition associated with being human and the like) but to be minimized and abolished, with the establishment of a more peaceful world as a key goal. Though some took issue with the metaphor, just as cancer was a problem for the human body, sometimes fatal, so war and violence were deemed to be a type of cancer within the body politic. At the centre of the endeavour was a problem: knowledge, therefore, was not for its own sake. What was needed was new knowledge addressed to an old problem. As Boulding put it 'It is not the noisy revolutions of politics but the silent revolutions of skill that change the course of man's destiny' (Boulding 1968 p.28).

Chapter 3

The Structure of Peace Research: From Invisible to Visible College

The evolution of a structured network of scholarship is seldom random (though in some circumstances it may be dependent upon chance encounter), but it is hugely significant in terms of how and why one set o f assumptions gives rise to or challenges another. The community of scholars, identified by institutional affiliation and membership in organizations, permits, allows and stimulates productive intercourse and changes in discourse. Nowhere is this more evident than in the area o f Peace Research. From the most modest of beginnings, Peace Research has grown, to the extent that the 1999 edition of the UNESCO World Directory of Peace Research and Training Institutions lists a total of 570. Making allowances for those included there that are more properly defined as departments of International Relations and/or Strategic Studies institutes, this still leaves a sizeable organizational nexus. More pointedly, the transition from the modest newsletter compiled by a small team, with willing student helpers, in the proverbial 'broom cupboard,' is no better illu strated than by reference to th e premises of SIPRI at Solna, north of Stockholm, and the proposed construction of new premises for the United States Institute of Peace in Washington, D.C.

If International Relations and Strategic Studies emerged with some visibility, and significant backing, at fairly specific times in relation to given circumstances, this is certainly not the case with regard to Peace Research. Its early emergence is a question of some dispute. Frank Barnaby (a former Director of The Stockholm International Peace Research Institute, observes that it emerged in the nineteen fifties. Adam Curle takes a rather idiosyncratic view in suggesting that Peace Research, from the perspective of the early nineteen seventies, was 'relatively new' and originating largely in Europe and particularly associated with the name of "Galtung"' (Curle 1971 p.3). Such an observation is indeed surprising, for he must surely have known of the work going on in North America whilst Galtung (and others) were at work in Europe. Indeed he was, but he chose to call these efforts, of Kenneth Boulding and Anatol Rapoport, 'studies of conf lict'. Richard Smoke asserts that 'since the mid nineteen sixties a b ody of thought and literature has appeared, not all of it basic research by any means, on reducing the incidence and effects of warfare, and of threats to security, by means other than by deterrence and defense' (Smoke 1975 p. 315). Pruitt and Snyder date th e formal inauguration of Peace Research as 1957, with the appearance of the Journal of Conflict Resolution, based at the University of Michigan. (Pruitt and Snyder 1969 p.x). John Burton notes, from a mid-sixties standpoint, that a range of new organizational initiatives were significant (Burton 1965 p.87). Cynthia Kerman noted that major efforts in Peace Research were not to come about until the period 1954-5 (Kerman 1974 p.68). Herbert Kelman dates the major initiatives from 1955 (Kelman 1968).

Does all of this matter? Why not take it as read that something happened around the mid-fifties – th e consensual view seems to s uggest that this is about right (and the title of this work suggests a concurrence with this view) – and simply proceed? Seeking for a p recise starting date is in itself probably futile and not important in itself. What is important is that finding a date from which we can say that Peace Research started will help us in two tasks: first, with respect to the question of status, we should be able to say something of the form 'in a period of this time and in these circumstances, Peace Research has achieved the following'. This would give us an idea of how long it takes to achieve significant results. Secondly, and related to the emergence of Peace Research itself, the precise origination of the new venture signifies the first stages of the shift from one paradigm to another. (In discussing the nature of scientific revolutions, Thomas Kuhn reminds us that most of the time, when doing research, we are s olving puzzles presented to us within an exi sting set of assumptions that are the foundations of knowledge in a given discipline or field of knowledge. We choose a topic, study it, say something of some significance (we hope) and fill in a gap. The probability of a Newton or Einstein emerging is remote, for it is with those sorts of individuals that we associate something revolutionary. We start to shift out of one paradigm and into another (Kuhn 1962). The collective efforts of the Peace Research pioneers did not produce revolutionary change, nor were they associated with but one individual, but they were significant, as we shall seek to show in due course).

But what about the question of relative invisibility? The work of Diane Crane is helpful in this regard for she demonstrates how new fields of knowledge emerge as an invisible college becomes more visible (Crane 1972). At first, individuals labour alone. They feel that they cannot accept the prevailing assumptions within their disciple: perhaps they are dr iven by a f eeling of discomfort, outrage or confusion. Something, somewhere and somehow seems not to fit or cannot be explained appropriately. There is a sense that something need to be done to sort out these paradoxes or m isfits. Usually, individuals are rel atively isolated in going about their work, especially insofar as they feel that they cannot share the widely accepted v iews (they may attract t he status of 'loner' within a department or s chool and feel that they are in a minority of one). But they then discover, to their profound relief that they are not alone. They may discover (and the advent of the Internet will surely have made this process of discovery more likely and swift, as opposed to the days of newsletters and the printed page, allied to what is now known as 'snail-mail') that a few others are sharing their sense of skepticism or conf usion. The individual in Calgary may find a lik e-minded individual in Canberra or C anterbury, or both and more. A network, private and invisible, evolves. If there is a significant sharing of concerns, the network may take on a s emi-formal status, perhaps sharing ideas and information through a newsletter (or, th ese days, a website). Gradually, the invisible and the isolated become more visible and collective, sharing and growing. All of these networks may not make it to the point of visibility since all id eas and agendas may not be shared. But the test of a good idea is that it is picked up by others, spreads and takes on a certain significance.

Those that do are significant. The next step is to go beyond newsletters to formal, and highly visible, journals. Then, perhaps, panels at con ferences and conferences themselves that collect together the interested and the like-minded. So do ideas evolve, whether they be in regard to Feminism, Post-Keynesian Economics, International Political Economy, Discourse Analysis – or Peace Research.

However, these initiatives seldom start from a tab ula rasa, as it were. The formal onset of organizations is also testimony to work done earlier. In many respects the formalization of the enterprise is the litmus test of the value of the earlier, pre-organization, efforts, not least because the early work appears to demonstrate not only that there is work to be done, but that it can be done. Building up a network represents the passing on of the baton to the next set of runners in the race for status and credibility. We should do well therefore to pay attention to the precursors of the Peace Research movement, for their work is not lacking in importance because it falls outside of our immediate gaze. A s Helge Hveem has\put it 'every historical phenomenon has its pre-history' including Peace Research (Hveem 1973 p.189).

We may divide the intellectual precursors into two types (and we have already hinted at this in the previous chapter); intellectual predispositions or value orientations and academic forerunners. Not entirely satisfactory, in itself, such a distinction at leas t draws attention to propitious circumstances within which academic initiatives have a chance of succeeding. The intellectual or v alue predispositions that preceded Peace Research include both pacifism, as a philosophical position, and Quakerism, as a reli gious commitment. In some cases these are not readily separable, but they are significant insofar as they both demand an articulation of answers to the question 'why war?' and 'how peace?' At the very least this involves sorting out distinctions: possibilities from passions, realistic responses from unconscious motives. The Quakers, for example, took the radical step of rejecting the concept of the just war, so central to the Christian tradition and 'as time went on, this rejection of violence became a "testimony", that is to say that it became a required Quaker attitude, and as the Society [of Friends] became more rigid the testimony became more of an abs olute requirement.' (Hubbard 1974 p.128). By way of an example we may cite the case of Kenneth Boulding whose commitment to Quakerism predated his firm commitment to Peace Research and whose personal history the link between one and the other. In earlier times, Philip Noel-Baker founded the Friends Ambulance Units in the early days of the First World War, campaigned against war until his death in 1982 and who was awarded the Nobel Peace Prize for his work 'The Arms Race' (Noel Baker 1958).

The pacifist position is well-known and its creed well documented (see, for example, Brock 1970 and Ceadel 1980) and is of interest here simply in view of the intellectual significance of the articulated pacifist stance which developed in Europe and North America. Moreover, it might be suggested that the pacifist position could be set in the wider context of thought frequently described as 'Utopianism' by some (see Manuel and Manuel 1979 for an extended discussion of this pattern of thought). By way of example, we may cite the case of Dick

Shepherd and the Peace Pledge Union in Great Britain and that of A.J.Muste in the United States. They were stances of opposition and rejection in light of the events of the First World War, and the assumptions that underpinned its causes and conduct.

Also in the period between the two World Wars the academic forerunners of Peace Research began the period of fertilization and early gestation. This process is associated with the work of Quincy Wright in the United States and Lewis Fry Richardson in Britain. And lest it be th ought that these individuals are i ncluded merely for the sake of completeness, we need to say emphatically, that without the work of these two individuals, the Peace Research movement could not have developed in the way that it did. The work of Wright and Richardson stood, and stands, as legacy, inspiration, pointer and stimulus to the further development of critical thinking about war and peace.

Wright, whose career was made in International Relations and International Law, was born i nto a family of pronounced scientific bent. His father is acknowledged as a pion eer of actuarial science and his brother, Sewell, was a pioneer in the field of animal genetics. A second brother, Theodore, was involved in the early development of aviation. Quincy, we are told, took the career path that he did feeling himself not capable of emulating his brothers. This is somewhat ironic, since, at the time of his death in 1970, Wright had been nominated for the Nobel Peace Prize. As an individual, Wright was inclined to s tudy the normative aspects of human behaviour, which helps explain his interest in the law. But, as an academic interested in science, by virtue of his family links, he was greatly influenced by the evolving code at the newly-established University of Chicago. It was here that the great American pragmatist John Dewey was working. So too was Charles Merriam, determined to provide a rigorous, social scientific foundation to Political Science and determined to take the subject beyond the then conventional formal analysis of constitutions and so on and institutional analyses and towards a more positivist and behavioural mode of analysis, at a time when such labels were far into the future. The presence in Chicago of a group of Logical Positivist philosophers, including Rudolf Carnap, was surely a key element in the new mood of rigorous analysis. (Also to emerge from this exciting milieu at C hicago were David Easton and V.O.Key Jr, who would have profound effects on the study of Political Science, in North America and beyond).

It was here that Wright embarked upon what was to become his magnum opus. 'A Study of War'. He began it in 1927 and it appeared in 1942. This is where Wright the normativist and Wright the scientist come together. 'A Study of War' (Wright 1965 Second Edition) is brilliantly encyclopaedic in its breadth and depth. The scholarship embedded in it is re markable. Here h e studies (and not indifferently) the phenomenon of war from several aspects – anthropology, history, biology, demography and so on. In introducing the second edition Karl Deutsch could write

That in 'A Study of War' 'he had brought together, with his collaborators a larger body of relevant facts, insights and far-ranging conclusions than any other man has done' and that 'he has done it n ot merely as a con cerned individual, though this would be enough, but as a s cientist. He has valued accuracy, facts and truth, more than any appealing or pref erred conclusions' (Deutsch 1965 p.xii).

Wright's study runs to 1400 pages, with a vast accumulation of statistical data, and it would be absurd to attempt a précis here. What is of more importance and simply stated here, are Wright's motives in undertaking the study. First, even before the development of nuclear weapons, he recognized that war was becoming more of a problem in an interdependent world; 'because the world is getting smaller, because wars are getting more destructive and because peoples are more impressed by the human responsibility for war, the recurrence of war has become more of a problem for a larger number of people' (Wright 1965 p.5). In that he was both accurate and perspicacious for in the decades after the Second World War, interdependence gathered pace, giving way to globalization, and wars – conventional and unconventional, declared and not declared, legal or illegal – became more and more of a problem for humanity. Secondly, he tried to see ahead to assess what might be needed to address this problem, concluding that 'Planning for peace cannot take place in the armchair. It can take place only in practical action to meet international problems. Such activity, however, will not contribute to peace in the long run unless its direction…is guided by a distant star and its details, however insignificant, are assimilated in growing world institutions, thus solidifying the gains that have been made' (Wright 1965 p.7). The significance of the work of Wright and Richardson, to whom we now turn, is that heir work was of direct value and importance in the founding of institutions and the development of the impetus to formal, institutionalized Peace Research in the nineteen fifties. To highlight we invoke the Rostovian metaphor (from W.W. Rostow's work pertaining to sustained growth and development in poorer economies), slightly amended: without the efforts of Wright and Richardson, the efforts of others notwithstanding, the Peace Research movement could never have achieved enough momentum to achieve lift and take-off into sustained growth after 1955. Indeed, Deutsch acknowledges this in suggesting that Wright's work 'on the study of conflict has been the pioneer of such later work as the continuing research by many scholars appearing in the Journal of Conflict Resolution and the Journal of Peace Research' (Deutsch 1965 p.xvi). And Deutsch's assessment of Wright is clear and unambiguous in its admiration for he suggests that 'in regard to the social sciences, the pursuit of knowledge about peace has gone unnoticed and unhonoured at the highest level. On the day on which this changes…mankind may well remember the pioneering contribution of Quincy Wright' (Deutsch 1965 p.xix).

Wright frequently makes reference to the works of Lewis Richardson in the statistical treatments in 'A Study of War', demonstrating both an intellectual debts and an affinity of concerns. As Wright was ploughing a lonely furrow in the United States, so was Richardson in Britain, and at a time when the rationalist-analytic approach to the study of war was distinctly out of step with the events of the time, where Fascism was evident in Italy and Germany and Hitler an important figure, giving rise to devil-theories of war and the nature of the totalitarian state and certain personality types. At the risk of overstating the point, such a stance as that adopted by Wright and Richardson must have called on great reserves of energy, courage and sheer persistence, qualities hardly consistent with the idea of a defensive mindset.

Lewis Fry Richardson came from a long Quaker line. The British social reformer Elizabeth Fry was from the same family line. He w as trained in the natural sciences and was a meteorologist and teacher (at the Paisley College of Technology, in Scotland) by profession. Richardson is remarkable in that he has two buildings named after him; the Richardson building at the Meteorological Office in Bracknell, Berkshire, and the Richardson Institute for The Study of Conflict (once based in London and now sited at the University of Lancaster). In his professional life he studied the weather. As a 'hobby' he studied war. This seems like a curious juxtaposition. What is the link between the two? We study the weather in order to u nderstand the nature of systems, their dynamics and their consequences for ourselves. We now have accurate knowledge of weather systems and very accurate predictions. In consequence, we take appropriate action; we do not don an overcoat when a heat-wave is forecast and we do not don a bathing suit when snow and frost are pre dicted. Richardson applied this logic to war, another 'inconvenience' for humanity. If we could see the phenomena with which war was associated, then we might be able to act accordingly, rather than be s ubject to its indiscriminate consequences. In other words, war was not to be treated as Providential, as we had long treated plagues of boils, locusts and famine: it was something associated with our being human and, thus something about which could learn – and act, do something about it.

As early as 1919 he had published a paper on 'The Mathematical Psychology of War', but his reputation, publicly at least, rests on the apperance of two works that were published posthumously, 'Statistics of D eadly Quarrels' and 'A Mathematical Theory of War' (Richardson 1960a and 1960b). In turn, as we shall see, these works provided a direct stimulus to further work. Richardson's work was not descriptive but analytical and rigorous. His Quaker inclinations and professional skills were conjoined as he addressed to questions not only of wars and quarrels, but also arms sales issues, amongst others.

The Beginnings of Peace Research

The year 1955 represents the onset of Peace Research in light of the conjunction of three separate events. Perhaps each alone could not have been sufficient, but each was necessary. Three constituent elements were brought together with synergetic effects. The three events in question were: first, the publication and reception of Theodore Lenz's work 'Towards a Science of Peace'; second, the formalization of a commitment to go forward with the organization of Peace Research, made a by a small group (a ' critical mass'?) at th e Center for the Advanced Study of the Behavioral Sciences at Sta nford University in California; and, thirdly, the publication of the Russell-Einstein Manifesto, a call for action by scientists in face of the proliferation and testing of more and larger nuclear weapons.

Yet before we proceed to discuss these, we need to have a clear s ense of the context within which they took place. The Cold War was at its most glacial. In the United States, militant anti-Communism was the dominant mood (on which see David Caute's analysis of the period 'The Great Fear' (Caute 1978) following the

Korean War, spy scandals (in the United States, Canada and Britain) and the consequent onset of 'McCarthyism'. The cultural apparatus that was to support visions of both the Cold War and 'the enemy' were in place an d cinema graphically portrayed the world in clear-cut oppositional terms. Good ex amples from the period would include 'Strategic Air Command' and 'The Invasion of the Body Snatchers' (sic) (see Biskind 1983). El sewhere, the Warsaw Pact had been founded in opposition to the North Atlantic Treaty Organization and specifically in response to the admission of the Federal Republic of Germany. This is not the place for an extended disquisition on the period, except to reiterate th at in was a period hardly auspicious for the initiation of peace-related work. What is especially significant is that this mood had effects upon what could be done and said. It is important to point out that where initiatives were taken in the fields associated with human behaviour, they were referred to as 'behavioural science', on the grounds that to call them social science would be ak in to ac knowledging that this was, possibly, on the way to Socialist science and therefore suspect.

Theodore Lenz, notwithstanding the claims of Richardson and Wright, has been called t he 'father' of P eace Research. Whether we quibble with the title or not, Lenz's role is crucial and his effects undeniable. To take but one, apparently unimportant, instance. In July 1962, ' The Guardian' newspaper carried a re port that referred to t he foundation of a P eace Research Centre in Lancaster 'founded by a Mr Pat rick Deighan, a Lancaster physiotherapist, after he had read a book by Dr Theodore Lenz'. We shall return to this in due course, for the Lancaster initiative was a se minal moment in the development of Peace Research in Britain. Lenz's work was based on a twofold assumption; 'the road to peace is not known, but it can be di scovered if enough of us make it our main business to look for it' (Lenz 1955 p.ix). Written over a period of six years, and representing the product of two decades of teaching and discussion, 'Towards a Sc ience of Peace' pointed out the extent to which modern culture had become unbalanced (in terms of values), how science had been misapplied (with a consequent discrepancy between social harmony and physical power) and identified the ideological impediments to peace. What he proposed was the adoption of a scientific attitude, united with key beliefs, what Lenz called 'articles of faith'. The first of these was in the possibility of human interests being harmonized. The second, that there was utility in facts that were still to be di scovered and that, third, these facts could be di scovered by the use of human intelligence. The fourth article of faith was represented in terms of a belief that research would evolve in accordance with the scientific method, since 'scientific research is a process in which developed curiosity makes utmost use of intelligence to formulate, develop, and progressively answer meaningful and relevant questions by the aid of purposeful observation and reason' (Lenz 1955 p.xiv). The fifth article of faith was a belief in the betterment of men as a u niversal goal, as opposed to personal or partisan betterment.

Lenz went beyond a mere summary of articles of faith, clearly believing that science and faith together were not enough. His analysis pointed the way in terms of how to organize Peace Research efforts to best effect and how to give priority to key issues. What is remarkable, in retrospect, is that Lenz saw the wider parameters of t he study of war and peace: he recognized not only the mercurial nature of peace as an idea (eas y to s ee, hard to pick up), nor only he massive problems facing the nascent study of peace. Mos t importantly, he answered the basic questions: how are we to do it? What are we to do? Insofar as he was aware of the need for organizational impetus, he went beyond the limits of the earlier reformers who had often pointed out the illogicality of a situation, but who had not been sufficiently well-organized to ef fect a s hift of log ic. Moreover, Lenz was quite clear that the intellectual basis of the new studies would have to be wide and draw upon the work of many researchers in disparate fields of endeavour, united in purpose but acting according to principles of division of labour. In short, Lenz was attempting to bring about the circumstances in which a ' critical mass' of researchers could come together organizationally and, having got to this crucial point, go beyond it in order to have an effect upon attitudes.

Whilst Lenz was working in St Louis, events wer underway elsewhere in the United States that would have the effect, combined with those of Lenz, to further the cause of Peace Research. In 1950 Herbert Kelman, then a social psychologist at Yale, had combined with Arthur Gladstone, from the Quaker Swarthmore College in Pennsylvania, to produce a 'Bulletin of Research on the Prevention of War'. On a small scale (and 'invisible') the Bulletin represented a forum for dissent and a means to disseminate research that was being done. In 1953 the job of editing the Bulletin passed to two graduate students at t he University of Michigan, William Barth and Robert Hefner, who 'were scrounging supplies and putting it out in a photo-offset format from the Psychology office' (Kerman 1974 p.68).

The year 1954 was the inaugural year for the Center for the Advanced Study for the Behavioral Sciences at Stanford; it was to be the social science equivalent of the Institute of Advanced Study at P rinceton, with the intention of providing facilities for scholars of established reputation, as well as ' junior' scholars. Amongst the latter was Kelman. One of the former was Kenneth Boulding (it was here that, in a matter of weeks, he wrote his classic 'The Image' (Boulding 1956)), who, though a faculty member at Michigan had not thus far taken much interest in the work of Hefner and Barth and the others that they had involved (including Daniel Katz from Psychology and Robert Angell from Sociology). Also at the Center in its inaugural year were Harold Lasswell, a political scientist and former colleague of Quincy Wright; Clyde Kluckhohn, an anthropologist; Anatol Rapoport, then a mathematical biologist, later to be a prime mover in Peace Research; and Paul Lazarsfeld, also a p olitical scientist. They were joined by Richardson's son, Stephen, who had brought with him the manuscripts of his father, only then available on microfilm, and with a limited circulation.

In these circumstances, Kelman called a meeting to dis cuss ways in which the 'Bulletin' could be i mproved. The effect of the meeting, in the mood at the Center, was to shift the study of peace to a new level. The stimulus of Kelman and the prestige of those assembled spawned an initiative to shift towards the publication of a journal. The prestige of those at Stanford seemed to make it easier to involve interested others of repute. In light of the organizational nexus, the journal was to be located at the University of Michigan and 'at a meeting in Ann Arbor, sometime in the winter of 1955-6, the title of the new journal was chosen' (Kerman 1974 p.69). The journal was to be cal led the 'Journal of Conflict

Resolution'; note that the word peace did not figure in the title. Or ganizational problems remained, however, regarding the production of the journal, as well as the vexed question of money. Graduate students are k een in the early days and come with the added v irtue that they are c heap – th ey cost nothing as they offer their earnest endeavours for free. In these circumstances, Boulding emerged to play a major role. Already, as a Quaker economist, Boulding had made significant contributions to the study of economics and, most notably, in 'The Economics of Peace' (1945) to th e analysis of the problem of war. In 1956 he obtained a small grant from the School of Graduate Studies and sponsorship from the School of Journalism at Michigan. At the same time, Boulding was responsible for a seminar series where ideas from a wide-ranging spectrum could be discussed. In 1956 the seminar series was devoted to the question of conf lict and many of the papers discussed there appeared in the first issue of the 'Journal of Conflict Resolution', which appeared in March 1957. There was now an identity, a v isibility and a collective enterprise.

Lenz, therefore, had initially publicized the idea of organizing the study of peace at a ti me when there were isolated pockets of endeavour, of th e type that Lenz wanted to see grow, but which needed a means to c oalesce into a greater, critical mass. With the changes at Michigan the mass became larger, though its future was not assured and its resources small and its status tenuous. The essential function that the Michigan group performed was to show that, even in an atmosphere of hostility and suspicion, the atmosphere so well described by Kelman years later (Kelman 1968), what Lenz had asked to be done was possible. Its function was thus exemplary; it would serve as a precedent for others elsewhere.

The third event 0f 1955 t hat makes it significant for our purposes concerns the call, from a wider and more prominent group of scientists, to address the problem of war as a matter of some urgency, for the survival of the human race in a nuclear age was at stake. Yet the response to this threat was not confined to initiative in 1955, f or a g ood deal h ad been done elsewhere. 'The Bulletin of Atomic Scientists' had been founded years earlier to re present, and act as a forum for, the views of those atomic scientists concerned at the role of atomic weapons and the threats that they represented. (Notable a mongst them was Josef Rotblat, who had worked on t he development of the bomb during the war but who had shifted his stance radically; thereafter he devoted his life to the problem of war and who, as head of the Pugwash Movement – of which, more later – was later awarded the Nobel P eace Prize. In the United States the 'Federation of American Scientists' had been formed, with a co unterpart in Britain, 'The Atomic Scientists Federation'. Much of t heir discussion was devoted to the responsibilities if scientists in the age of nuclear confrontation.

On the individual level, the American pacifist A.J. Muste urger Albert Einstein to make a public plea in favour of the newly-formed Society for Social Responsibility in Science in 1950. In response, Einstein addressed his scientific colleagues and argued that not only did the Society serve a need, but that 'through its discussion of the objective problems confronting the scientist, it will make it easier for the individual to clarify his own mind and arrive at a co nclusion concerning his own actions. Moreover, mutual help is essential for those whose situations will become more difficult whenever they act according to conscience' (Nathan and Norden 1960).

Why is this important in terms of the development of Peace Research? The movement to organize the collective conscience of the natural science community represented a shift in organized opinion, not of soft-headed Idealists, but of people of science and, therefore, authority. The significance lies in the fact that these men and women, many of whom had been in the vanguard of developments in nuclear physics, sought to minimize the impact, for ill, of atomic energy, by means of the impact of moral suasion, backed by the authority of science. Were they merely lay individuals, then their protests and concerns might simply be dismissed as rather lightweight. That they were men and women of authority and social status gave them a voice too loud to dismiss.

As early as December 1945 Bertrand Russell had called for a meeting of scientists from both Western and Soviet blocs to discuss the threat to civilization posed by the atomic bomb. Russell, ever the iconoclast and attacker of shibboleths could have been regarded as something of a figure of fun, one of the 'usual suspects; except that his reputation as a mathematician, philosopher and social critics gave him some status and authority. Moreover, as Ronald Clark reminds us, the views of Russell were shared by military men. (It is worth noting at this point that many formerly high-ranking officers joined in the vocal criticism of the deployment of nuclear weapons in Europe in the 1980s; once out of uniform and role, they seemed free to voice their opinions, as we shall see later). In December 1954 Russell broadcast on the B.B.C. on the subject of 'Man's Peril' and cited the comments of Sir John Slessor, former Air Force officer and innovator in nuclear thinking, to the effect that 'a world war in this day and age and would be general suicide' and the even more alarming conclusion of Air Marshal Sir Philip Joubert, who argued that 'With the advent of the hydrogen bomb, it would appear that the human race has arrived at the point where it must abandon war as a continuation of policy or accept the policy of total destruction' (Calrk 1978 p.670). In summary, Russell was being joined by other authoritative sources to suggest that the Clausewitzian logic of war – as a continuation of politics by other means and long central to the conduct of international politics – was now a central problem and not a legitimate means.

In 1954 Russell wrote to Einstein, in the wake of the B.B.C. broadcast, 'which made a great impact on public opinion' (Rotblat 1972 p.2) and asked him to join in the publication of a manifesto, which stressed the need for agreement between East and West to reduce tension and the need for the abolition of nuclear weapons. The Manifesto, published in July 1955 and signed by Einstein only two days before his death, concluded with a resolution to the effect that , in light of the dangers represented by nuclear weapons, 'we urge the governments of the world to realize, and to acknowledge publicly, that their purpose cannot be furthered by a world war and we urge them, consequently, to find peaceful means for the settlement o all matters of dispute between them' Signatories of the Manifesto were mostly Nobel Prize winners, among them Born, Bridgmen, Pauling and Joliot-Curie. 'The press', according to Rotblat, 'gave the manifesto excellent coverage, with the result that hundreds of letters and cables, from individuals and groups, came pouring in from many countries, expressing approval and offering help. It was evident that the Manifesto had touched a sensitive chord in the minds of the public and scientists: that the idea that scientists should take an active part in world affairs had the approval of public opinion' (Rotblat 1972 p.2).

This, too would have cumulative consequences. There were also offers of finance, certainly sufficient to enable a meeting of scientists to take place. The Indian Prime Minister, Nehru, offered to play host, but nothing came of it. So, too, Aristotle Onassis offered to host a conference in Monte Carlo. Cyrus Eaton had enthusiastically offered help to Russell after the publication of the Manifesto and, after the plans for the Delhi conference fell through, it was decided to accept Eaton's offer of finance and hold a conference of scientists at Pugwash, Nova Scotia, Eaton's birthplace. Such were the origins of what came to be known as the Pugwash Movement, a series of reguar conferences that united East and West, even in the most difficult times of the Cold War. In due course they would come to involve social scientists, even military men of high standing in the east. The first Conference took place in 1957 and the Pugwash Movement continues to this day, now also a Nobel Laureate, in effect.

Evidently, between the reception of the idea of a recurrent series of conferences (and, later, specialist workshops) and the start of the process, much work needed to be done. Rotblat (1972) has provided us with the information as to how this was done, he himself having played a central role. The significance of Pugwash, for our purposes, is that it demonstrated that, even in the glacial conditions of the Cold War, initiatives were not only possible but deemed desirable. Not all took this view, of course, and many critics took the view that many western organizations devoting themselves to discussions of peace were obviously full of Communist dupes and stooges. Nevertheless, Pugwash served as a model and, later, John Burton, (an Australian who had been both a senior civil servant and briefly a diplomat) who joined in many of the later Pugwash conferences, was to take the initiative in forming the International Peace Research Association as a type of social-science Pugwash.

So, here are the key initiatives that came together to give decisive impetus to the nascent Peace Research movement. Where did it go from there? That it has survived when so much was ranged against it is itself notable and stands reiteration. That it has grown is impressive. The extent and rate of growth might be seen by a comparison of the various editions of surveys conducted by the United Nations Educational, Scientific and Cultural Organization (UNESCO). The first of these was conducted in the mid-sixties and they have been conducted at regular intervals since. By 1966 there were 81 institutions recorded as doing work classified as Peace Research. This had grown to 149 by 1973 and 310 in 1978. The most recent report shows even further growth, with the total approaching six hundred. Even allowing for a degree of self-classification, where institutions say that there are doing Peace Research type work (but which include, for instance, Departments of International Relations, The Royal Institute of International Affairs and the Department of War Studies at King's College London), growth is self-evident and the trend is upwards.

We need not dwell on the numbers here. Anyone wanting to find out the state of play nowadays has at t heir disposal a h ome computer and access to one of several search-engines. 'Peace Research' will be a tu rnkey to many sites that interlock, some being compendious and serving as directories of what is going on in the field.

Doubtless, there will be those who see the glass half-empty, while some will see it as half-full. What is beyond doubt is that the spread and rate of growth of Peace Research have been uneven and we must address this to see why this should be so. In some cases, there is evidence of regression, with research institutes becoming smaller and even closing down. Evidently, Peace Research has been closely associated with developed regions of the world which have achieved high standards of living an where there are funds to permit large-scale research. In other words, we should not be surprised to find that the bulk of the institutions are to be found in the United States and Europe. But we should not let this observation pass without comment, for we can immediately recall that the milieu within which the American initiatives took place was hardly conducive to radical change. What matters here is that the decade of the sixties saw radical changes in American social movements and, consequently, prevailing values. In a ti me of war, peace came to be a cause for activists and lifelong commitment, often to research and scholarship. But this is to get ahead of ourselves.

But the growth of Peace Research is not merely an agglomeration of national styles and attitudes, nor is it about, only, key individuals. We have argued the case for seeing Peace Research emerge as an invisible college becoming more visible and, in becoming more visible, more organized and, therefore, rather less reliant on the decisive roles of key individuals and willing graduate students. Over time the complex organizations tend to become more complex, dynamic, with a 'corporate' identity and an evolving agenda. Adopting his perspective works from the basic assumption that there was some degree of informal organization, that national institutes do not exist in isolation (that there is a co llectivity of like-minded scholars, identifiable as such and known to each other through their shared concerns: even if we do not know our colleagues personally we do know them. In due course, conferences and workshops allow us to es tablish contacts. And, of course, just as much informal diplomacy gets started in the corridors of the UN in New York or the EU in Brussels, so it is that many books and research projects get underway at conferences, well away from the formal sessions that attract us in the first place.

So, how did the emergent and growing corpus of interested individuals begin to organize itself? What factors were crucial? Which initiatives were important? What follows is not a comprehensive treatment of every how? and why? involved here, but is a sample view of where institutes and organizations have developed and, by and large, succeeded. The survey that follows helps us to ex plain where and how Peace Research has been stimulated and supported and where it has been suspect. In some places where we might have expected some significant developments, it i s almost wholly absent. Nevertheless, where it h as succeeded these institutes and centres have succeeded, not only in doing Peace Research, but disseminating it a nd claiming for themselves a v oice too important, and authoritative, to miss. In doing so, they have made Peace Research less of an imposter or cuckoo in the nest and more a legitimate and, now, valued field of scholarship.

We have already referred to the stimulus represented by Lenz's work insofar as it was an inspiration to individuals behind the Lancaster initiative in Britain. The Lancaster group was informal and privately funded. It 'produced a roneoed [an early form of reproduction] newsletter, circulated to several universities, in which they reported seminar discussions, reviewed books and commented on world news' (Hickie and Elliot 1971 p. 1). In London, at about the same time, a group of concerned natural scientists, including Professors Jack Mongar and Cedric Smith at University College, formed together to discuss questions of war and aggression. Hickie and Elliot draw a distinction between the aims of the Lancaster and London groups; the former wanted action, the latter academic enquiry. (Hickie and Elliot 1971 p.2). In fact, it proved difficult to involve universities in the processes of Peace Research at this early stage, owing to the relatively backward state of the social sciences. Whereas, in the United States, there had been a massive and widespread growth in the social sciences, which might at least be thought conducive to its development, this was not evident in Britain. Perry Anderson's (Anderson 11992) account of the components of national culture at this time is suggestive of reasons why. As Anderson reminds us, virtually the slowest universities in Britain to accept as legitimate the discipline of Sociology were Oxford and Cambridge, despite the fact that it had been respectable in the United States since the foundation of Albion Small's department at the University of Chicago in 1890. The general point to be made here is that the widely held view was that matters of war and peace were adequately studies within the fields of history, philosophy and the like. Even International Politics was still a relative newcomer.

However, the landscape was not entirely bleak and there were signs of convergence. The Ciba Foundation had been established in 1945 to further research into questions of biology, health and medicine. In the early 'sixties its Deputy Director, Anthony de Reuck, initiated a shift towards the social sciences and, in so doing, involved some members of the small London group, whci were looking at conflict as an aspect of human behaviour. In effect, new or existing institutions, led by individuals known by sight or reputation, began to emerge and coalesce. One outcome of the process was a conference held in 1963 at Cumberland Lodge, Windsor. Publicisation and promotion of the emergent bases of conflict research took place and 'by 1964, after the Windsor conference, there was a network of people interested in furthering peace research in an academic framework' (Hickie and Elliot 1971 p.3). John Burton soon became involved in this process when he arrived in London in 1964 to teach International Relations at University College. This is not the place to review Burton's life and work since it has been done elsewhere (Dunn 2004), but is pertinent to point out that Burton had great experience of international diplomacy and foreign affairs. He was a former head of the Australian Department of External Affairs and had attended the founding conference of the United Nations at San Francisco, amongst others. He was now an academic in London, but he brought with him a book, 'Peace Theory' (Burton

1962), his experience of the Pugwash movement and a personal commitment to get things done. Consequently, some were to find him rather abrasive and over-direct. Not all did and he received Quaker support when taking his early initiatives.

Under the auspices of Ciba a symposium was organized and its proceedings were published in 1965 with the title 'Conflict in Society' (de Reuck and Knight, 1965); it was later translated into German by Dieter Senghaas. Of this work it has been said that it 'remains one of the first authoritative works in peace re search' (Hickie and Elliot 1971 p.3). Participants included Kenneth Boulding, Anatatol Rapoport, and Harold Lasswell (all, recall, pres ent at S tanford in 1954-5), Johan Galtung, Herbert Marcuse, Bert Roling and Karl Deutsch. Two organizational initiatives followed: first was the decision to try to establish Peace Research in a university environment and , s econd, a du al plan to organ ize Peace Research professionally in Britain and found a j ournal. By 1964 t he Conflict Research Society was founded in London and in the following year the newly-established University of Lancaster created a P eace Research fellowship, at the same time that the Lancaster Centre was receiving financial support from the (Quaker) Cadbury Trust and the Nuffield Foundation.

The initiative to develop a centre in the south of England passed to Burton, in conjunction with others. But before we turn to that, it is appropriate to turn our attention to Pugwash. What was it? What did it actually do? And who went to its meetings? Burton attended three conferences up to 1966. Philip Noel-Baker attended seven, Robert Nield two, Kenneth Boulding three, Rolf Bjornerstedt two and Hannes Alfven two (for a fu ll list of sessions and participants, see Rotblat 1972 pp.91-106). It was more than an example; it actually addressed matters of moment and bridged the much-discussed cultural divide between the social and natural sciences. Moreover, it was also topical in it s discussions; topics for discussion included 'Problems of Disarmament and World Security' (1962, 1963 and 1964), 'Disarmament and Peaceful Collaboration Among Nations' (1964) and 'International Cooperation for Science and Disarmament' (1965). In smaller and more specific workshops the question of anti-ballistic missile defence was discussed in 1968 and the implications of new technologies for the arms race in 1970. Each, of course, were central to the policy agenda at that time. In sh ort, Pugwash was both exemplary and relevant.

Burton wanted to follow this example. The Ciba Foundation Annual Report for 1964 n oted that 'a group of social scientists, including sociologists, social psychologists, historians and international lawyers met at the Foundation (in London) from 1st to 3rd December to h old a C onference on Research on International Peace and Security, convened by Dr J ohn Burton, along the lines of the Pugwash Conferences'. This is confirmed by Hickie and Elliot, who add that the plan to establish CORIOPAS (**C**onference on **R**esearch in **I**nternational **P**eace **a**nd **S**ecurity) , directly related to policy, met with some disapproval from Rotblat, who argued that CORIOPAS would be political in intention, as compared to Pugwash which, according to Rotblat's conception of it, was apolitical (Hickie and Elliot 1971 p.4). In fact, the move to establish CORIOPAS was unsuccessful, but the real outcome of t his series of dis cussions was the foundation of T he International Peace Research Association, in 1964. In augural members of IPRA were Norman Alcock (who had established the Canadian Peace Research Institute on a s mall scale), Robert Angell (from Michigan), Elise Boulding (Kenneth's wife), Tony de Reuck (from The Ciba Foundation), Johan Galtung (from the Peace Research Institute at Oslo), Walter Isard (from the Department of Regional Studies at the University of Pennsylvania, which became, in due course, the base for the Peace Science Society (International), Bert Roling (from The Polemological Institute, Groningen), Alan Newcombe (from TheCanadian Peace Research Institute) and Rotblat, from Pugwash. The small were now joining together to greater effect – a nd with more visibility. Not s urprisingly, at t his stage, most of what was being done took place in Europe and North America.

IPRA persists to this day. Indeed, in 1989 i t was awarded the UNESCO Peace Education Prize. It is global in reach and is now served by a series of regional associations. It meets every two years at venues across the globe and thrives. (see, for further information, the IPRA website). In addition to its regional associations IPRA also has a series of functional/specialist commissions, such as the one on Peace Education, the total of functional commissions now totaling twenty. Indeed, it n ow has its own IPRA Foundation and is endowed with funds (commemorating Paul Smoker and Kenneth Boulding) to fund research. In 1996 a new journal was launched 'The International Journal of Peace Studies', in association with the regional commissions of IPRA.

IPRA was not the only organization to emanate from the Burton initiatives in London. As well as being instrumental in the formation of IPRA, Burton was now teaching International Relations at U niversity College, London. Necessarily, as a teacher he had to ground his approach within the the-conventional wisdom: it was still dominated by a state -centric paradigm and, within that paradigm, the Power Politics approach dominated. Burton was soon critical of the conventional wisdom and began to move through it, as it were, in search of an alternative frame of reference. He sought to explain conflict but without the vocabulary and assumptions of the power frame of reference. He attracted sufficient funding to establish The Centre for the Analysis of Conflict, based at Un iversity College. Amongst the first staff at t he CAC were Michael Nicholson (the first Peace Research Fellow at Lancaster), Michael Banks (who was teaching International Relations at the London School of Economics), John Groom (a col league of Burton's at U niversity College), likewise Christopher Mitchell, and Bram Oppenheim (from the Department of Social Psychology at the LSE, where a small group had studied conflict, along with Roger Holmes, who would play a part in the evolution of the Conflict Research Society). A number of continuing conflicts were studies by the group at the CAC, where Burton brought together representatives of parties in conflict to see if resolution could be effected. Out of this experience came a significant body of literature principally from Burton (Burton 1969), Frank Edmead, who had joined CAC later (Edmead 1971) and a collective effort from Burton and some of his London colleagues. The principal point to make here is that the work that initiated in London in the 1960s is now being followed through in many areas of Peace Research, as it too ev olved, encompassing not merely the arms race, deterrence and the like (the early concerns) but also expanding the agenda as events themselves and new academic initiatives coalesced and fed back, to IPRA and elsewhere. Peace Research was to be dynamic and relevant – or it was to be nothing. In North America in 2005, there are scholars working on further amplifications and implications of the work started by Burton (see, for example, Kelman (1986), Montville (1997), Fisher (1997) and Saunders (1998).

In 1970 the London and Lancaster arms of Peace Research came together. Paul Smoker (whose move into Peace Research had been directly stimulated by Lenz and who had been involved in the early work of the Lancaster Peace Research Centre) had become established – after returning from the United States, in the Peace Studies Programme at t he University of Lancaster, now exposing students to evolving peace th inking in the context of postgraduate training. Nicholson moved from Lancaster, to C AC and then to becom e Director of the 'research wing' of the Conflict Research Society, the Richardson Institute for Conflict and Peace Research. In its time in London, the R ichardson Institute attracted a v ariety of scholars. Andrew Mack (later h ead of the Peace Research Centre at the Australian National University in Canberra) was, for a time, Deputy Director. Notable v isitors from the United States included Bruce Russett (later Editor of the 'Journal of Conflict Resolution', when its base moved from Michigan to Yale) an d Cynthia Enloe (a pion eer in bringing the emergent Feminist approaches closer to In ternational relations and Conflict Research). Adam Curle also spent a year at the Institute as a Research Fellow preparing work for 'Making Peace' (Curle 1971), before he went on to becom e the first Head of the new Department of Peace Studies at the University of Bradford. Dan Smith, later head of PRIO in Norway, was also a R esearch Fellow. It was a repos itory for work done, with a g rowing library and archive (including Richardson's own manuscripts, on an extraordinary range of subjects), a f orum for seminars and discussions and a meeting place. Nevertheless, it was never adequately funded and moved back to the University of Lancaster at the end of the 1970s. The archive was sent to the University of Kent, to which Burton and Groom had moved at the start of the seventies, and it became the base for a slightly reduced CAC. The Conflict Research Society persists, indeed expands, attracting a new generation of scholars and holding annual conferences.

However, it was not all a picture of gloom for, in 1974, Bri tain's first Department of Peace Studies was established (with cross-party political support, it should be n oted) at the University of Bradford. The Department was small at the outset and, in a ti me of strained university finances across the sector, some expected that it would be first for 'the chop' if cuts had to be made. It was new and some even questioned whether 'Peace Studies' actually amounted to anything, save a trendy name and a woolly core. But it did initiate undergraduate course in peace studies, as well as postgraduate degrees. It survived, prospered and is now a vibrant source of exciting works being done in Britain. Its student body is large, drawing in young undergraduates and mature professional from varied niches in society. However, apart f rom Bradford, cu rrently in Britain only Lancaster and (not surprisingly) the University of Ulster represent significant Peace Research presences. In other universities, individuals work within Departments of International Relations. The dominant culture, with regard to matters of war and peace, is that of International Relations and Strategy.

Of France, there is little to be said, since there is almost nothing being done in France in this area under the rubric of Peace Research. Here, the cultural and academic paths lead elsewhere. The dominant figure of post-war France, Raymond Aron, still cast a long shadow over discourses of war and peace, largely within a geo-political frame of reference. There is a sm all presence, but no input to the literature that truly demands attention. However, it would be foolish to omit mention of the work, and influence, of Michel Foucault in the last three decades. Foucault's many and varied works engage with questions of power relations in society, the rendering of individuals as objects rather than subjects, the marginalization and incarceration of others and so on. Though he does not share explicitly in the discourse of Peace Research, what he has to say is akin to work done by Galtung (specifically the notion of structural violence) and Burton (particularly in regard to the manner in which societies frustrate the fulfillment of human needs, coerce individuals into conformity and marginalize those who refuse to do so, labeling them deviant in the process. (Rabinow 1984 is a particularly useful introduction to Foucault's work).

If the British example shows rather mixed trends, the picture in Scandinavia is extraordinarily different. All was not plain sailing in the early days. Johan Galtung had enormous difficulties establishing the Oslo Institute in the nineteen – fifties. Circumstances there were not auspicious as Galtung tells us looking back; 'Today it is strange to think back to those early days of 1959. "What a terrible word!" was the spontaneous exclamation of a leading official of the Ministry of Education when the first whispers of "Peace Research" started circulating. In those days "peace" was considered a word from the left, politically subversive or at least naïve, scientifically unfashionable, even indicative of incompetence' (Galtung 1975 p.13)

In fact, there was no avalanche of financial support, perhaps not surprising in light of the preceding remark. But there was some. Sigmund and Eric R inde provided $5000 and support for an Oslo Institute. A smaller cash grant came from Otto Klineberg (an associate of Lenz in the United States) of whose work on international understanding Lenz hade made note (Lenz 1954 p.iv). Initial funding was a harbinger of more in due course and the Norwegian Ministry of Education stepped in to encourage the foundation of a 'Council for Research on Conflict and Peace' and the NAVF (Research Council) came in with support for specific programmes. After a lengthy transition – i ndeed, what Galtung called 'a considerable fight' (Galtung 1975 p.17) – the University of Oslo established a Chair in Peace Research. Financial support permitted the dev elopment of an administrative infrastructure and subsidized the foundation of a j ournal. But to Sigmund and Erik Rinde asserts Galtung, the one a director of a research insitute and the other a director of a business company, and from abroad came the means to break the circle of lack of money, summed up by Galtung as follows; 'unless you have proven yourself we cannot give you a grant; unless you have a grant you cannot prove yourself' (Galtung 1975 p.17). N ot only did the Oslo institute survive, it has prospered to be an institute of global importance. It is responsible for a wide-ranging research agenda, again dynamic and relevant, has been a haven for visiting scholars and is also responsible for the publication of the 'Journal of

Peace Research', arguably the major European journal in the field. Galtung's career has seen him visit universities and institutes too numerous to mention. His output alone is prodigious and we shall return to him in due course.

Galtung and PRIO were important in forging links with the UN s ystem, principally UNESCO. The first UNESCO repertory of Peace Research institutions was carried out by Galtung for UNESCO and the second was the responsibility of the staff of PRIO, under the supervision of Nils-Peter Gleditsch. By 1980, Galtung had moved from Oslo to bec ome associated with the United Nations University Project, first in Geneva, and, later, with the World Order Models Project (WOMP) associated with the Institute for the Study of World Order in   New York and associated with Saul Mendlovitz and Richard Falk. The link to th e UN system might be seen as a move towards the 'collective legitimization' of Peace Research by the members of the United Nations, in this sense. The UN s ystem of states, much altered through the process of decolonization, has evolved different norms and values as compared to the system that comprised only fifty states at the end of the Second World War. Some have seen this trend as irksome and irritating, others as necessary and legitimate. But, given that context is itself an important influence on what gets discussed and studied – a nd why – t hen the engagement with the collectivity of states is a means not only to legitimize the enterprise but also to maintain a position of relevance to emergent concerns.

At the UN Special Session on Disarmament in New York in 1978 (itself an indication of a changing agenda), one of the organizations contributing to the discussion was not a s tate, but a res earch institute, the Stockholm International Peace Research Institute (SIPRI). SIPRI stands as a supreme example of a case not of government support, but sponsorship of Peace Research.

The idea for the foundation of an institute like SIPRI began to emerge in light of discussions relating to appropriate ways to mark Sweden's 150 years of unbroken peace, which anniversary was to be   marked in the mid-sixties. In December 1964 a Royal Commission was established by the Swedish Government to investigate the possibility of establishing, in Sweden, an international institute for peace an d conflict research. The Commission was chaired by Alva Myrdal, who was at the time (and had been for many years) involved in UN efforts devoted to peace and disarmament. Later still she would become the Swedish Minister for Disarmament and a recipien t of the Nobel P eace Prize. Also members of the Commission were Hannes Alfven, a professor at the Royal Institute of Technology in Stockholm and a participant in Pugwash, and Karl Birnbaum, the Director of the Swedish Institute of International Affairs, amongst others. The Commission submitted its proposals in 1966, af ter 'consultations...with international organizations and with scientific institutions in different countries' (Statens Offentliga Utretnigar (SOU) 1966 p.57). The Commission deemed the establishment of the Institute both possible and desirable and was mindful of the need to make the institute international in character and capable of adding a new dimension to P eace Research. The recommendations included also that the institute's work 'should be primarily directed to the problems of disarmament and arms regulation' and that studies 'should be of an applied character' directed to questions of practical politics and carried on with an interchange with research of a more theoretical kind (SOU 1966 p.59).

SIPRI was established on July 1st 1966, by act of the Swedish Parliament, which supplies funding direct to SIPRI. It has developed rapidly since then and moving from a location in central Stockholm to a larger site in the suburb of Solna. It has published a Y earbook annually that notes, with authoritative data, arms transfers, arms control measures, proliferation issues and the like. Here is the emphasis on the problem of armaments and a direct relevance to practical concerns. In addition, it has sponsored a s eries of multi-year research projects (attracting scholars from all parts of t he globe) which in turn have given rise to a series of monographs on topics such as, inter alia, nuclear weapons proliferation, the arms trade, the arms race at sea, chemical and biological weapons, weapons and their effects upon the environment, the law of inhumane weapons, space technology and resource questions and security. Undoubtedly, though, SIPRI stands for more than this. For some it will stand as an authoritative store and source of data, not provided by their own governmental infrastructures. Its secure funding also permits a wide dissemination of its work, now assisted by the advent of the internet.

As with Pugwash, SIPRI is exemplary, but there are c loser links. It i s tempting to suggest that the Swedish Government and Pugwash were responsible for the foundation of SIPRI. Of the members of the investigating Commission, Hannes Alfven and Karl Birnbaum had been involved in Pugwash. Robert Nield, the first Director of SIPRI, was involved with Pugwash, as was Frank Barnaby, the second Director and a former member of the Pugwash Secretariate. Of the staff at SIPRI, Theodor Nemeth, a C zech, had been in Pugwash from its inception. The Governing Board of the Institute had involved, at one time or another, Bert Roling, Leo Mates and Rotblat from Pugwash and the Scientific Council has included Philip Noel-Baker, Kenneth Boulding, Johan Galtung and Ala Myrdal. What was, arguably, invisible in Pugwash achieved clear visibility in SIPRI. For s ome of them, it represented the fruits of their labours. For others, it demonstrated what was achievable.

There is also another link. As members of the Scientific Council of SIPRI, in 1971, Lord Louis Mountbatten and Sir Solly Zuckerman participated in the direction of SIPRI. Each brought a di fferent perspective; Mountbatted from an experience of military matters in Britain and NATO, Zuckerman from his experience as a former Chief Scientific Advisor to the British Government. By the late 1970s, both were to emerge as vocal and articulate – and credible – c ritics of the prevailing nuclear orthodoxy. To an unknowing public, their intervention in the debate, with Noel-Baker, might seem unusual. In light of their links at SIPRI in the preceding years, it appears less so. What had gone on before m attered and they were informed and authoritative. Mountbatten was assassinated in 1979 bu t, in December 1980, Zuckerman and Noel-Baker, together with Sir Michael Carver (a former British Field Marshall) articulated their concerns over nuclear weapons to a general meeting held in London – and organized by Pugwash!

It is also important to pay attention to the development of Peace Research in the Federal Republic of Germany, for here too the evidence of government support is conspicuous. In a report of a survey carried out in 1975, the Secretary General of the United Nations commented that 'Universities and scientific institutes in The Federal Republic of Germany are increasingly turning their attention to peace and conflict research' (UN General Assembly, 1975 p.49). Dieter Senghaas had made a similar observation two years earlier and suggested that a transition process was in motion, pivoting around the turn of the sixties into the seventies (where the German political authorities were pushing forward the policy of Ostpolitik, seeking to change relations with eastern Europe for the better and when, in 1970, the Federal Chancellor, Willy Brandt, knelt in front of a memorial in Poland; until the end of the sixties, he observed that what work that was being done was on an individualistic basis and that 'there was no real public debate on Peace Research as a science and on Peace Research as a necessary prerequisite for peace policy, nor were there funds for research' (Senghaas 1973 p.161). Apart from the observation about the 'state of play' at the time, the comment is notable for its articulation of the objectives of Peace Research.

In June 1969, the newly-elected Federal President, Gustav Heinemann, publicly expressed the need to address peace as a major issue, or 'the emergency' as he put it. He then proceeded to suggest that 'it would be very helpful if we could direct our attention to Peace Research; that is, the scientific analysis not only of the interconnections between armaments, disarmament and peace strategies, but also the interrelationships between all f actors including social, psychological and economic ones'. Interestingly, he then went on to suggest that the agenda should not be constrained by the prevailing Cold War oppositions of East and West but that 'we should look [at] the North-South conflict' (Senghaas, 1973 p.161). Surely such comment of worthy of note, not just for what is being said but for who said it. Is it not remarkable that a major figure such as Heinemann should speak of Peace Research as he did? In the German situation of the time, perhaps not as remarkable as might be first thought. West Germany was divesting itself of a militaristic past and the legacies of defeat in two World Wars; feeling itself delicately poised between East and West, indeed as a p otential battle-zone (with NATO strategists developing responses to potential Soviet pressures on Berlin, surges through the Fulda Gap or attempts to claim Hamburg in a swift attack); now economically well-developed, a res ult of the 'German Economic Miracle,' and reconstructed; with a vocal and articulate population (and an especially critical student body); and policies of Ostpolitik and détente. In other words, the issue of peace as a social value was thrust to the centre of public debate. Research on peace was therefore directly relevant and valued for that.

Significantly, therefore, one of the primary areas of research for the German Society for Peace and Conflict Research (DGFK) was the strategy of peaceful transition in Europe (UN General Assembly 1975 p.49). The Society had been founded in 1970, f ollowing relatively swiftly on from the Heinemann initiative, and the 'principal political and social groups in the Federal Republic of Germany are represented in the Society's organs' (UN General Assembly 1975 p.49). Senghaas observes that the Society was founded 'thanks to great efforts by some politicians and researchers' with the idea of promoting not only Peace Research but also the idea of peace. L ocated in Bonn-Bad Godesberg (i.e.close to the centre of government) had close links with the Federal and Lander governments, as well as social and political groups. Thus, 'More than any other Peace Research organization, this Society has from the very beginning stressed the perspicuity of its research promotion policies' (Senghaas 1973 p.162).

Within the first four years of its foundation, the DGFK received Bert Roling and Johan Galtung as visiting professors of Peace Research. In this context, we might note that these, and others, brought experience and authority to the infant German organization, as well as impetus and organizational links to Oslo, IPRA and beyond.

Nor was the DGFK initiative the only one in the Federal Republic. In fact, it had been preceded by an initiative at the region/Land level since the Prime Minister of Hesse, Albert Osswald, in conjunction with scholars, had founded the Hesse Peace and Conflict Research Foundation (HSFK) based in Frankfurt. Thus, the HSFK 'became the first major Peace Research Institute within Germany' (Senghaas 1973 p.162).

Perhaps the Germans enjoyed a rather surprising advantage, relative lateness. There had been hard-learned lessons elsewhere, from which the German pioneers were able to learn. They were able to add weight to their own skills by bringing in authoritative figures like Galtung. Moreover, there was curious mix of intellectual crosscurrents swirling around at the time in Germany, a mix of American social science, Scandinavian Peace Research, German philosophy and Marxist scholarship, not to mention Critical Theory. Interestingly, too, the Swedish Nobel Prize-winning economist Gunnar Myrdal (husband of Alva) offered a cautionary note when he suggested that 'I cannot abstain from expressing my wish that...German Peace Research will not, as so often in the American setting, seek escape into a stratosphere where it does not disturb policy managers' (Myrdal no date p.19). Not only was this a call to keep German Peace Research 'honest'; it was also a significant swipe at the American Peace Research movement, now into its second decade. We now turn to a consideration of the nature of the American experience, but before we do so it might be pertinent to make a remark about the past and the present. We commented earlier that the Germans had sought to escape from a militaristic past. This has now been accomplished. It was therefore remarkable that, in the search for allies in the prelude to the invasion of Iraq in the Spring of 2003, certain voices within the United States Administration voiced their concern not only at the emergence of 'Old' and 'New' Europe, but that the Germans, in particular, had become rather pacifistic! We might entertain the notion that the experience of Peace Research in Germany might have had something to do with this transformation, as well as the public opposition frequently expressed in Germany on matters of defence and security (most notably I the context of the NATO decision to deploy Pershing and Cruise missiles in 1983). That aside, the German example is a useful and illuminating example, set against the British, where a social valuation of peace thinking and sufficient funding are significant aids to growth. In Britain, by contrast, limited funding and a different social context make growth limited at best and contraction not impossible.

It is to the United States that we now turn, not only in light of the pioneering efforts of the fifties, but also because in all of the surveys of Peace Research being done, the vast majority of it is being done there. That the society of the fifties gave way to the radically different society of the sixties and after is cen tral to this growth. The Civil Rights Movement showed that spaces could be opened up in a conservative, conformist society and the Vietnam War ensured that those spaces for alternative debate were exploited to the full. Only in light of the Vietnam conflict can we explain the growth of Peace Research in the United States, from modest beginnings. But this is but one factor among many, though it may have been decisive in explaining the rate and scope of growth.

In some respects, the growth of Peace Research in the United States is easily explained; in others it i s more difficult. The initial efforts to es tablish Peace Research met with resistance. We have already noted the role of the small Stanford group and the efforts of Lenz in St Louis. Yet 'peace' was greeted with some suspicion. Only with great difficulty was the 'Journal of Conflict Resolution' established, in the Department of Journalism at Michigan. Shortage of funds immediately threatened the survival of the Journal and, in fact, the editors had taken the decision to discontinue publication after three issues since no more money was forthcoming. However 'there came a phone call from a woman to whom Bill Barth (responsible for fund-raising) had talked earlier. She had a small foundation and decided to give her last thousand dollars of foundation money to the Journal' (Kerman 1974 p.70). The continuation of the Journal saw a shift of efforts to es tablish a res earch centre. Again , th ere were problems. 'There was active resistance from the faculty of the Department of Political Science, most of whom felt that international problems were their province...and some of them cherished an unfulfilled dream of a Center of their own' (Kerman 1974 p.71). An anonymous donation of $65,000 d ollars, to be u sed for the purposes of Peace Research, enabled the University of Michigan to establish the Center for Research in Conflict Resolution, in 1959. It survived until 1971. Many of its supporters had moved to newer institutes or universities and funding was not forthcoming. However, for Rapaoport, at least, the Center had had a major impact, stimulating the efforts of others (Rapoport 1978). Shortly afterward, the editorial base for the 'Journal of Conflict Resolution' shifted to Yale University.

So much for the initial organizing push, Why, then, rapid and significant growth? In the late sixties, Mackenzie suggested that money had been an important factor in the growth and dominance of American political science, permitting large research projects and exploiting the capabilities of computers to store and manipulate large data bases (Mackenzie 1967). But Peace Research was hardly over-endowed with funds. Yet a s econd issue related to money in the American context; there is a long tradition of priv ate foundations disseminating funds to appropriate causes, either in the way of large grants, or in establishing named centers or professorships for specific purposes. This is hardly developed in Britain and represents a significant sociological difference; in Britain, only one or t wo family-based foundations provided support and amounts, though certainly significant and much appreciated, they were not vast.

There is also the question of the pragmatic theme in American social in American social thought. This is most often associated with the philosopher and educationalist John Dewey, but there were others who preceded him, not least the (for long) relatively unknown Charles Sanders Peirce. This approach put great store on the relationship between knowledge and action, purpose and consequence. This has to be set in relation to a comment by the eminent historian Richard Hofstadter, particularly one of his most important books 'Anti-intellectualism in American Life'. Published in 1963, the work surveyed the role of intellectualism in American society and Hofstadter proclaimed that 'particularly in recent years it has been noticed that intellect in America has been resented as a kind of excellence, as a claim to distinction, as a challenge to egalitarianism, as a quality which almost certainly deprives a man or woman of the common touch' (Hofstadter 1963 p.51). Yet the years preceding the publication of t he book were the conformist conservative years of the Cold War, where there was little space for intellectualism, not least because there was a s hared view of the world; the coomonly held view was obviously the democratic United States versus the totalitarian Soviet Union. That, obviously accurate, and widely-shared view needed no further articulation or investigation.

The sixties changed this. By 1971 K enneth Keniston could write that 'the new campus hero is the professionalist (Keniston 1971 pp.99-126). (Moreover, university campuses had been sites of 'sit-ins' in protest at the Vietnam war.) On the question of professionalization, an important by Thomas Haskell is illuminating. His work is based on a stu dy of the rise o f the American Social Science Association, from its foundation in the 1890s (also the period of dramatic innovation at the University of Chicago). For Haskell, the rise of the ASSA is vital in understanding the 'rise to cultural dominance of the social sciences in the late nineteenth and early twentieth centuries' (Haskell 1977). Though that 'dominance' was not to last, it was to give rise to a code of professional ethics, standards and procedures in American social science widely defined, with disciplines evolving their procedures for conferences, conventions, meetings and newsletters. In other words, when Peace Research did gain a critical momentum, there was a clear code of practice with respect to where it was to go, how it was to do it an d what procedures were to be followed. Above all, American Peace Research sought to be professional and authoritative.

To repeat, there can be no more stark contrast between the 1950s and 1960s in the United States . There was a cum ulative process of s ocial change and, for much of the sixties, critical debate an d protest were the prevailing norm in many sectors of society, not least the universities. Many of those involved in protest saw this as a l ife-changing stance and, undoubtedly, many went on to found and teach in the many Peace and Conflict or P eace and Justice Studies programmes in Liberal Arts colleges and larger universities. Writing in 1976, W ehr and Washburn prefaced their own survey of institutions by arguing that 'the past decade has been characterized by, above all, a crisis of institutions…The Vietnam experience has brought about a change in American public consciousness and attitudes. There is, we believe, a much expanded "peace-attentive-public" as a result of the Vietnam War, and more elected repres entatives willing to c hallenge assumptions of executive policy-makers' (Wehr and Washburn 1976 pp.1-2). The scale of the field in the United States is indeed remarkable.

So too is reco rd of the campaign to establish what was called the National Peace Academy. The National Peace Academy Campaign (NPAC) began in 1976, the aim being to establish an academy which 'would teach meditative skills for use at community, national and international levels. It would also sponsor, coordinate and carry on research in this vital field (NPAC no date). Members of the Executive Council of the NPAC were Elise and Kenneth Boulding and Herbert Kelman. Also extremely prominent in the Campaign was the Senator from Hawaii, Spark Matsunaga. In June 1977 th e U.S. Se nate passed a bill (S 469) to   create a commission to s tudy the proposals for a U.S . Academy for P eace and Conflict Resolution. In Congressional hearings preceding this decision, evidence on the need for an academy was presented by Herbert Kelman and David Singer. Singer's enthusiasm was tempered with caution; he argued that much work needed to be done, but scientifically. 'We definitely need one agency that speaks for conflict resolution and conciliation, but that voice must reflect scientific knowledge, rather than another conventional wisdom or body of folklore' (House of Represeantatives 1978 p.330). Recall again, Boulding's categorization of folk-, literary- and scientific-knowledge. What Singer was surely asking for here was that the new institution should not just be a v ehicle for a reiterati on of the old order's assumption: it should deal with the new knowledge evolving. Kelman argued the case for independence, saying that though the new body would be F ederally established and funded, it should 'function essentially as an independent public corporation' (House of Representatives 1978 p.231). In addition, evidence was presented by representatives of the International Peace Academy, based in New York. Funded by governments, the IPA was funded by governments who paid tuition fees to send diplomats, military officers and policy planners to various training programmes in peacekeeping and peacemaking. As such, the vice-president of the IPA told the House subcommittee its work – is aimed at t he practitioners, rather than the theorist'. Nevertheless the President of the IPA, General I.J.Rikhye, a former UN peacekeeper, argued that the IPA 'has supported

   Domestic efforts around the world to improve the quality of practical conflict resolution education' (House of Representatives 1978 p.97).

   Legislation was passed in 1979 (after several unsuccessful attempts, it should be noted) to establish a Commission on Proposals for the National Academy of Peace and Conflict Resolution. The Commission was chaired by Senator Spark Matsunaga and heard submissions from many interested parties, the testimony finally running to 6,000 pag es. A Final report was issued by the Commission in 1981, positively recommending the foundation of an academy. An Act founding the United States Institute for Peace was signed into law by President Reagan in 1984 and the Institute began work on 17th Street, NW in Washington. In recent years a site has been chosen, together with an architect, for a purpose built Institute of Peace, on The Mall in Washington, D.C. Funds for the project are being sought, to allow the construction on a site well-nigh unmissable to visitors to, and citizens of, Washington, D.C. Visibility indeed.

Chapter 4

The Journals:
The Means of Peace Research

In the preceding chapter we have dealt with the organizational development of Peace Research. In this, shorter, chapter we turn to a consideration of the journals. This might seem a trivial, perhaps unnecessary survey, but it is frequently the case, in discussing why and how disciplines and field of study develop, that academics are seldom explicit about why they do what they do. They research, teach, write and submit articles to 'professional journals' since this is apart of their professional code of conduct. Some journals are accorded status above others, but most are the means to make ideas public and subject to professional scrutiny. An idea poorly received by one's peers is seldom developed.

But why are there more journals? How can their growth be explained? Again, the professional code has much to with it, since it become increasingly the case in recent years that academics are encouraged to do research. Frequently, universities are awarded extra funding and status in light of their performance. In Great Britain, in recent years, the Research Assessment Exercise has been a particularly salient feature of the academic process. We might expect, as a consequence of increased pressure to publish (or perish?) that this would lead to more journals. And so it has. Many add to the literature of the mainstream, whether it be problems in the European Union, NATO expansion, the changing foreign policy agenda, dilemmas for the World Bank and so on.

But many are innovative, as Peace Research has sought to be from its inception. The significance of the journal, as an instrumentality, is highlighted by Kuhn. As he puts it 'formulation of specialist societies' is but one sign of the shift out of one paradigm into another. Two other signs of development; the formation of specialized journals and the claim for a special place in the curriculum (Kuhn 1962 pp.18-19). The claim for a special place in the curriculum will be addressed in the next chapter, when we have engaged with the substantive content of Peace Research. At this stage we are concerned with two dimensions of the journal question; first, their appearance, in time and place and, second, the question of content. However, we are not concerned with an article-by-article content analysis. This is beyond our scope. What is significant is an idea of the general trend and direction the journals take. What, after all, are the new journals saying that is not being said elsewhere? What constitutes their essential novelty and role?

The first issue to be addressed is what we mean by 'specialist journals'. This is not merely a semantic point. What concerns are being engaged, by those with special skills, that allow them to publish in journals or record and authority? Before the appearance of Peace Research, explicit attention to matters of war and peace were confined to the discipline of International Relations, with the defined problematique (i.e. t he shared sense of what it was 'about', the foundational paradigm) of order and stability in a system of states devoid of central authority. Two broad approaches could be discerned; on the one hand the so-called 'Realist' position, that sought to order and stabilize the system, through the exercise of power and influence; and, second, those, termed 'Idealists', who sought to improve the prospects of peace and order in the system through the exercise of reason, law and the harmonization of int erests. To repeat, Idealis m and Realism represented different approaches, but they could both be located in a given paradigm, the ste-centric system, where there was no higher authority than the state and where the system of states was essentially self-regulating. This was what was taught, learned, absorbed and guided research in the field. It was an ethos represented in the corpus of knowledge contained in journals such as 'International Affairs', 'Foreign Affairs' and 'World Politics' for example.

In the field of strategic studies, the elements of power, control, order and the military aspects of international relations were predictably more pronounced. This concern was reflected in the journals of record, such as 'Orbis', the 'Journal of Strategic Studies', 'International Security' and 'Survival', though this does not exhaust the list. In matters of domestic politics, there is again a clear a genda to be addressed, whether this be el ections, comparative government and the like, as in, for example, 'The American Political Science Review' or the British journal 'Political Studies'. Clearly, all these journals have sought to move 'with the times' since the times have changed so radically and rapidly, hence our earlier extended discussion of context. However, on the whole, few of these journals have been congenial in terms of their reception of Peace Research. This is not to say that they have not welcomed the occasional article from time to time. But they have not, in general terms, reflected the assumptions and concerns of the alternative approaches to peace and conflict (at all social levels) represented by Peace Research.

This is not in itself surprising; editors always receive more material than they can publish. Journals tend to reflect a consensual view, perhaps through a policy of balanced content, of a regi on, discipline or prof essional group. Novelty is not necessarily a virtue, and is often received with skepticism: sometimes a key article can shift the grounds of debate radicall y. In these circumstances, the need for a journal outlet, within which new and different things can be expressed is obviously important, indeed vital, not only as a means of visibility, but also of as a means of legitimizing the new field and seeking to ensure its continued existence. AS such, a journal is not a des irable adjunct to an evolving movement: it is a necessity, and without it th e movement for innovation would be less eq uipped for the task f innovation. In the age of the Internet, it may be that emergent groups will find that the role of the journal is overtaken by the website, not only to disseminate news of events, but as a means of publication for new work or, i ndeed, as an electronic library, with internet publication instead of the printed page medium.

The importance of the role of the journal was highlighted by Galtung, on both practical and 'philosophical grounds', when he argued that the commitment was made to a less-violent world, with violence being conceived of broadly; 'for that reason the research effort was spread over many fields and resulted in many articles rather than a few books on, for instance, a theme like East-West conflict alone. There was also a practical reason, not peculiar to Peace Research: the article form shortens the time period between research, publication and feedback considerably' (Galtung 1975 p.13).

Holsti, an International Relations scholar of some standing, argues that books may be considered the 'more considered' thoughts of an author, and there is clear merit in this view (Holsti 1974 p.218). It is not a question of either/or; the well-received article for a journal can be the foundation of a good book. A collection of articles that are valued and have stood the twin tests of criticism and time may be constituent parts of 'readers' or collected es says, to appeal to a wider audience before the appearance of 'the textbook', that work which is a distillation of the endeavour, the essentials of what it is ab out, that which can be taught, to advanced undergraduates and perhaps first-year undergraduates. Of 'the text' Kuhn says that 'the applications given in the texts are not there as evidence but because learning them is part of learning the paradigm at the base of current practice' (Kuhn 1962 p.80).

Before moving to a discussion of the journals, and at the risk of getting ahead of ourselves, it is pertinent to point out that those who began to study something that came to be called 'Peace Research' and 'Conflict Resolution' (we shall explore the significance of the labels later), for maybe two generations, started out on the quest from somewhere else. For e xample, John Burton started in International Relations, Kenneth Boulding in Economics and Johan Galtung in Sociology. There is now evidence that the efforts of those who came from other disciplines to found a new one are reaping the fruits of their labours, in the sense that there are scholars and practitioners who went straight into Peace Research and Conflict, to learn its basic assumptions, acquire and contribute to the further articulation of the new paradigm. And, thus, representing the results of research done within a new paradigm, learning from the new journals and methodological and substantive insights contained therein?

The Journals: A General Survey

In asserting that there are differences in content and style between established and new journals, we must acknowledge that there are 'grey areas' at the margins of the debate. John Burton wrote from an International Relations perspective but rapidly moved through that discipline towards conflict resolution (Dunn 2004). He had earlier ex plored the relationship between International Relations and Peace Research (Burton 1965). David Singer straddled the divide between the two, contributing to the empirical content of both but clearly playing a pioneering role in Peace Research (see Singer 1965 and 1968). Similarly, Karl Deu tsch, Bruce Russett, Anatol Rapoport and Richard Falk have straddled the divide and Chadwick Alger has served as head of both the International Studies Association (the premier professional organization for International relations in the United States) and head of the International Peace Research Association. The

'International Studies Quarterly' is rooted in the ISA and, according to Chatfield, is 'a journal through which new paradigms are being explored which are multi-disciplinary, multi-level and integrative of domestic and international processes'. Which may be the case as International Relations has sought to cope with the porous nature of state boundaries and the inter-relationships between domestic and interstate agendas. However, this debate has spawned a search for new approaches, models, and theoretical initiatives, perhaps searching for paradigms new but not, even yet, finding them. The ISQ is a medium for debate about the relative merits of these emergent novel schemes, but it is surely hard to sustain (then or now) that 'the ISQ must be accounted the major broad-grouped organ of Peace Research in North America' (Chatfield 1979 p.173). Many Peace Researchers would not see it as such, nor would many in International Relations, one suspects, welcome such a label.

The 'Journal of Conflict Resolution', as we have seen, first appeared in 1957, with enthusiasm and a little money behind it, with an insecure future but a clear objective; 'to stimulate and communicate systematic research and thinking on international processes, including the total international system, the interactions of governments and among nationals of different states, and the processes by which nations make and execute foreign policy. It is our hope that theoretical and empirical efforts in this area will help in minimizing the use of violence in resolving conflict'. We should take especial note of the way the problem being addressed is constructed. The focus was on international conflict, especially where violence was used, allied to the question of foreign-policy making. There was to be focus on theoretical and empirical work and 'on the basis of interdisciplinary work and action' (JCR 1957 vol. 1.1 p.1). Perhaps there is little new here in terms of states and foreign policy as a focus of attention. But the stress on processes is significant, as well as domestic influences on foreign policy: to challenge the then-prevalent notion that domestic concerns were for political scientists and foreign affairs for a different set of specialists?

But what of the stress on interdisciplinarity? International Relations, founded in 1919, could hardly be described as exhausted in the 1950s, but perhaps it was limited in terms of what it could (and could not) explain. It too had drawn on other disciplines and was classically 'eclectic.' In another major work, which appeared in 1955, Quincy Wright looked at the eclectic nature of International Relations and identified a series of what he called 'root disciplines', including law, anthropology and so on (Wright 1955). But these root disciplines were being drawn on on to help analysts deal with the central problem of understanding the relations between sovereign state entities, where they lived side by side in a system of self help and where the prime consideration was the achievement of order, sustained if possible. The classic dichotomy, for many in International Relations, was as between order on the one hand and justice on the other. But this was almost always resolved on the basis that the achievement of order should address the issue of justice, as a means to an end. If it were a case of order or chaos, then chaos would render justice impossible. If order could be achieved and maintained, then at least the question of justice could be discussed as a (long-range) goal. Recall, too, that conflict was thought to be endemic in the system and violent conflict was not outlawed, though a legal framework within which war and force might be used had evolved in some degree.

What Peace Research sought to do was to stress the violent nature of the system and put violence, war and conflict at the agenda's centre. To that extent, the pioneers saw that the Peace Research agenda was problem-centric, rather than issue- or actor-centric. The fact that they sought also to be interdisciplinary is a de facto criticism of the assumptions, capabilities and knowledge-base of International Relations. Of course, it could not ignore International Relations, but it also sought to bring in findings from psychology, social psychology, anthropology, mathematics, game theory and the like, to further illuminate the processes that gave rise to war in the international system. Which is not surprising given that, at the time the project started, this was the overwhelming problem: the prospect of thermo-nuclear war and the possible extinction of the human race. In time, the question of violence and conflict would take on a wider meaning.

So what are we to make of 'eclectic' and 'interdiscplinary'? Eclecticism means drawing on other areas in order to enrich our own existing perspective on a given social realm. So, a scholar of International relations might fraw on science and technology to examine the nature of modern weaponry and how this affects deterrence; or might draw on economics to illuminate aspects of economic security and vulnerability of states. Interdiscipinarity suggests something both more far-reaching in its goals and perhaps agnostic in its means. Agnostic in the sense that nothing was ruled out, a priori, as being more or less relevant to the problem at hand. There was no implied hierarchy of inputs: a scholar from International relations had no necessary prior claim to have a 'better' claim to authority than a scholar from, say, psychology or the emergent field of ethology. The problem was war and conflict, psychology and perception, the manner of us as against them. Disciplinary source was no barrier to a scholar making a contribution, save that that contribution should be relevant, systematic, perhaps empirical, but always rigorous. In this sense there was an implied task, not just of attempting to be far-reaching, but also of open-endedness and constant adaptation of the task of encompassing new findings, with a process of inherent task expansion as a modus operandi. There was no obvious point at which it would be possible to say that we have drawn on others subject enough, so that we can now, with authority, concentrate on our own particular concerns. In the matters of peace and conflict, they existed in a world ever-changing, throwing up novelties and problem that made any sense of establishing a boundary-fence (if one were even necessary or desirable) well-nigh impossible. This is not an invitation to anarchy, nor is it to say that 'anything goes' because anything can. Rather, it is to say that the Peace Research enterprise is interdisciplinary and problem centric. As a mature enterprise it may even be a-disciplinary.

From its earliest days, the 'Journal of Conflict Resolution' reflected its times in two ways. As to the engagement with the substantive concerns of the day, it focused on arms races, deterrence, perception, images of the enemy, negotiation, crisis behavior and so on. These were the dominant concerns of the day, of that there could be little doubt. In the second sense, the early peace researchers were keen to establish what it was that they were about. Thus, there were numerous articles on the nature of the field, its relationship to other disciplines and the central elements of its own agenda, substantively, methodologically and, significantly, as to its statu s (extant or in the future) as an 'applied science' rather than as an enterprise that could accumulate knowledge for its own sake. Could Peace Research be 'applied.' Recall, this was at the time when the social and behavioural sciences were much preoccupied with the nature of ' value-freedom' and 'objectivity' as key issues in the move to make social science more 'scientific' and rigorous. From the perspective of the twenty-first century and after the influences of post-modernism and its various offshoots and interpretations, some may think this an endeavour entirely Quixotic. But in seeking to establish the social sciences on a firm foundation, capable of separating information from argument and analysis from exhortation, the question of the 'participant-observer' was necessarily important (see, for example, Meehan (1965)). And even in the period after postmodernity, we still face the question, if not out and out relativism, then what? By what authority, criteria and methodologies are w e to offer advice on questions of public policy? Presumably, systematic gathering of information, rigorous interpretation and authoritative, reasoned presentation of argument are still essential elements of the task. This is, after all, what we ask of our students.

When the 'Journal of Conflict Resolution' moved to Yale in 1973, Bruce russet said that it would still be concerned with work that was 'hard-nosed' and theoretical (Russett and Kramer 1973). With this there seems, on the face of it, little with which to ta ke issue. The Journal has published a good deal of material that is theoretical, heuristic and exploratory in purpose and it has long had an interest in questions associated with the more 'formal and mathematical approaches to the issues. But critics did take issue with this chosen approach, and forcefully. In 1976, for example, Reid and Yanarella argued that the Journal had evolved 'into a techn ically oriented, value-obscured and theoretically vacuous organ and the virtual elimination of methodological pluralism and political debate by the mainstream figures in the field (which) symbolized the capitulation of this refuge to the dominant tendencies of the social sciences and the techno-corporate state (Reid and Yanarella 1976 p. 316). This is, indeed, a dam ning criticism and there is no smoke without fire. Without doubt, Peace Research had moved on in two decades, as it surely should have done: what was at issue was that some critics felt that it had, as far as the Journal of Conflict Resolution was concerned, moved in the wrong direction. Recall Gunnar Myrdal's comment, quoted earlier, about the engagement with the stratosphere.

Nor were Reid and Yanarella, writing within North America, alone in criticizing the direction of Peace Research. If they directed their critique towards a particular journal (perhaps as a repres entation of the whole or a g reater part thereof), critics in Europe, often younger scholars, were also vocal in their dissatisfaction. As van den Bergh argued Peace Research 'should contribute not so much to increasing knowledge that can enhance control possibilities of specific states or political movements, but to increasing the possibilities for as many people as possible to more realistically orient themselves in the world in which they live' (van den Bergh 1970). Oth er critics of similar cast included Schmid (1968) and Olsen and Jarvad (1970). Significantly, Peace Research was changing, but so was the world to which it sought to be relevant. The decade of the sixties had seen the emergence of the New Left, vocal about not only the war in Vietnam, but also about the conditions of capitalism as the post-war decades gave way to affluence, but also to what John Kenneth Galbraith had identified as 'private affluence and public squalor' (Galbraith 1954). The achievements of capitalism were an issue, domestically and internationally. The European empires had fallen and given way to a wave of de-colonization, except that the experience of de-colonization had was more apparent than real; neo-colonialism was now the subject of debate. So too were the conditions of subservience, both in domestic societies and internationally, most notably in the works of Franz Fanon (see 'The Wretched of the Earth', 'Black Skin, White Masks' and 'Studies in a Dying Colonialism') and Albert Memmi. It is incontrovertible that works such as these, and there were many, were not only required reading on their appearance, but instrumental n terms of the effects that hey had in changing much of the public consciousness in the West, certainly amongst aware and articulate sections of public opinion, including academia.

In drawing attention to the conditions of the relatively powerless, this wider constituency was actually engaging with work being done within Peace Research. Johan Galtung had shifted the debate away from the question direct violence, the infliction of direct pain, harm and suffering on other people, to a wider agenda, which he termed 'structural violence', which could be defined as the infliction of violence on others by virtue of their place in a given society. Thus, the poor ad dispossessed, insofar as their status was due to the dynamics of, say exploitative capital, then a form of violence, that condemned them to servitude and poverty, was being inflicted upon them. In these terms, he argued, there could be no such thing as a happy slave, for the condition of slavery was incompatible with the state of happiness.

Much of Galtung's work appeared in the 'Journal of Peace Research,' which first appeared in 1964. It was the first European journal in the field, with its editorial base at the Peace Research Institute in Oslo. Galtung was its first editor and it was he who articulated its guiding ethos; the journal was to be about research, but it was also to go further, to encompass what might be called 'peace search'; that is, 'an audacious application of science in order to generate visions of new worlds, closer to GCP (general and complete peace) and to suggest policies. What can make it peace research would not be empirical confirmation but theoretical consistency. This applies to analyses of Peace Research itself'. He also stressed the international and interdisciplinary character of the enterprise and argued strongly that it should be problem-centric. This would allow disciplines and research tools to be brought to bear as were necessary and consistent with the goals of Peace Research, its problems and concerns. There was alo a clear statement of what was required: 'What should be avoided are discussions that are merely programmatic and bring nothing new in theory and/or data, or discussions that are merely conceptual or t axonomic and hence contribute nothing in terms of hypotheses or propos itions. And discussions should have relevance for peace policy; one should try to state explicitly – if only in general terms – what kinds of policy one would favour as a consequence of the findings made' (Galtung 1964 p.4).

Several of these points need amplification. First, Galtung mentions the need to be au dacious in terms of the visions of a future world. This means that there would be (and still is) a need to be essentially creative, making leaps of the imagination in constructing visions of peace. This might be co mpared and contrasted with the stance of incrementalism, moving slowly and cautiously from where we are to where we want to be. The two stances are complementary. But the stress on creativity need even further stress. As Mary Clark was to put it, decades after Galtung's stated aim for the new Oslo journal, 'the conditions of what is possible are not static' which comment is preceded by an anecdote, told to h er by her father-in-law, who ran a pub in England. A man came in seeking the road to Ipswich (a long way away); he was advised by a local farmhand 'Well, if I wanted to get to Ipswich, I wouldn't start from here.' (Clark 2002 p.374). This is not to be glib or avoid the difficulties of where we are; i t is to suggest that sometimes our assumptions and working frames of reference are confining us, as if in a conceptual jail. And, to compound the point, Galtung himself wrote a bo ok about future security systems in Europe, long before the Berlin Wall fell, with the title 'There are Alternatives!' Doubtless many thought that this was a book akin to many another 'Utopian' tract, interesting but not relevant, on the grounds, self-evidently, that the Cold War would persist and the Berlin Wall would stand as a symbol of the great divide. Ex cept that the divide en ded, much to t he great puzzlement and astonishment (and embarrassment?) of many experts in International Relations and Strategic Studies who failed to predict or anticipate the series of events that came with such suddenness and profound consequences. Which, presumably, made Galtung's set of alternative futures for European security a degree more relevant and, arguably, validated the approach that he had adopted.

Secondly, Galtung saw a role for empiricism, but argued also for theoretical consistency. Clearly, a s cientific endeavour that seeks status and rigour demands evidence, properly accumulated and interpreted, with a th eoretical frame of reference to make sense of data, which, after all, d oes not 'speak for itself'. The 'facts' are n ot self-evident, requiring that we be s ophisticated in terms of methodology and the grounds for interpretation. But Galtung also makes much of what he calls theoretical consistency. This need not imply that any attempt at 'theory' should always and at every stage be rooted in the data and evidence. There is also the prerequisite for consistency in the bases of conceptual development and rigorous analysis of what is being suggested and why. What is being suggested in a novel framework that cannot be ex plained within the limits of the old? To take, briefly, one example. John Burton, in trying to explain the incidence of conflict in societies, argued that a d ominant code of conduct, on the part of authorities at all levels of society, was to try to control and repress or coerce th ose who challenged existing norms and values. Where they were not so controlled, they were classed as deviants and treated accordin gly. The operation code was prevention. Burton turned this notion around, stressing that, rather than causing individuals to conform to society (often with dysfunctional consequences and at great cost), societies should adjust to the needs of individuals. In this, he was being entirely consistent in moving from the limits of one concept, prevention, to the potential effects of a new concept, prevention. A further stage of testing the validity of the provention framework is to turn to empirical testing. (Burton 1990) Pu re induction is not without potential, but its value is at b est limited; in mature science, we need to be looking for something to test, not something to leap out at us.

Thirdly, he directed that question of theoretical consistency inwards towards Peace Research itself. The point, presumably, being that peace researchers should be, as a matter of course, critical of s elf and others, reflexive and relating work done to the aims and objectives of the endeavour itself. Implicit in this is the notion that self-reflexivity is an open-ended process, pushing us forward, never to reach an end-state, but steering us towards a comprehensive process of adaptation. Not least because the concept of 'peace' is not to be defined in terms of a fix agenda of criteria, to be ticked off, so that we know when we 'get there', to peace. We never get there, for we live in times of change. Context is all, reflexivity is crucial. Relevance is the link.

Also based in Oslo, and first appearing in 1970 u nder the editorship of Marek Thee, was the journal 'Bulletin of Peace Proposals,' the overriding aim of which was 'to present systematically, to compare and discuss in the light of general peace theory [which it was clearly now assumed to e xist after t wo decades of work] various plans, proposals and ideas for justice, development and peace' (Thee 1970 p.3). Especially notable here is the inclusion of development (and the lack of it, presumably) as a key component of t he agenda, stemming directly from Galtung's notion of structural violence. This new bulletin represented an extension of the Galtungian argument presented in the Journal of Peace Research. Why, asked Galtung, in the first issue of the new journal, a new one of this nature, concerned with peace propo sals? Three reasons were given. First, there was a pragmatic need of a distinct kind, for peace propos als to be av ailable and systematically presented. This, it was argued, 'would speed up, if only a little' the application of peace propos als. The second reason was educational; 'to shift attention 'more towards the solution of a conflict, less to the genesis and dynamics of the conflict'. In saying so, Galtung was stressing the need that research ought to be more purposive and rather less analytical. Moreover, in saying as much, Galtung offered a direct and explicit criticism of work already done. Too much of the analysis, he said, was too deeply rooted in the pasts of conflicts and 'we feel that the tradition of searching for a solution to a conflict in te past is too deeply interwoven with traditional moralism expressed and institutionalized in religious, legal and political thinking and organization. Since guilt can be distributed only if past and present behaviour are adequately ascertained and evaluated relative to pre-existing standards, accurate and adequate descriptions of pas t and present are always called for. This largely ex[plains why historians and lawyers have had such a dominating influence in the general field of in ternational relations and the 'Bulletin of Peace Proposals' should be seen as an effort to create a better balance' (Galtung 1970 p.6).

The third reason given was to stimulate research on proposals for peace, not least in order that such research could be made more legitimate. The point cannot be overstated. In International Relations and Strategic Studies, there is a premium on dealing with the here and now, as opposed to futures. Both have conspicuously lacked, until relatively recently, a con cern with long-term futures (and perhaps even short-term too), an d this is entirely consistent with the immediate and proximate task of ensuring order in a violent world that, potentially, teeters on the edge of chaos. Thus, order now is an over-riding consideration. In shifting to a stress on proposals, Galtung was seeking to shift away from a time-bound analysis of current concerns only, in order to invest the field with a sense of vision and creativity. He was at pains to point out that working on future-orientated proposals was more difficult than working with data In this, he was mapping out a series of proposals that were also central to the World Order Models Project (associated with Saul Mendlovitz and Richard Falk) and to which project he also contributed. Needless to say, Falk et. al. were greeted with skepticism by many working within the confines of the conventional wisdom.

These are generally regarded as the major journals in the field, certainly in the early days, but they are not the only ones in a niche that is still expanding. The journal 'Instant Research on Peace and Violence' first appeared in 1971, based at the Tampere Peace Research Institute in Finland (which is now associated with theReasearch Institute for Social Sciences at the University of Tampere, TAPRI having been founded by the Finnish Parliament in 1969). Little or nothing has been said here about the developments in Finland and Denmark. What we can say is that their appearance is not surprising, nor is there persistence in countries which exist within areas of long-term stability (the Nordic Union), in areas of some sensitivity, where a con cern for peace m ight be j udged important in terms of wider social discourse (Finland) and where traditions of social democracy and welfare have elevated certain key socio-political values that place a priority on peace politics. The Journal was designed as 'an interdisciplinary and international journal of scientific reports in the field of peace research. The journal concentrates on actual problems and phenomena related to questions of war and peace. It deviates from the ordinary kinds of scientific journal in stressing less methodological aspects and concentrating more on results obtained'. (IRPV 1971). In 1978 the journal name was changed to 'Current research on Peace and Violence' 'due to the fact that, for those who did not see t he journal for themselves, the earlier name evidently conveyed a misleading image of its content and quality' (Vesa 1978). The point at issue here is less the name and more the objective; to make work done instantly/ soon available to inform public and a wider academic debate.

'Alternatives' is a journal associated with the World Order Models Project and first appeared in 1975. Though not, in the strictest terms, a Peace Research journal, in terms of its orientation. Nevertheless, its aims are consistent with that of Peace Research and, over three decades it has shown consistent overlap with those scholars who see Peace Research in a maximalist sense, as the presence of peace being more than about the minimization of international violence. Issues of justice, dignity, identity, norms and v alues and wider aspects of academic/cultural discourse are notable in th eir coverage. 'The main purpose of the journal is to promote wider-ranging discussion and debate on the future of the world from the perspective of a set of values. Principal among these values are autonomy, and dignity of the individual and of peoples, equality and justice as principles of social organization, participation in political and economic decision-making structures and in the productive process, elimination of oppres sion and coercion in human and international affairs and harmony between nature, man and technology. The journal will be normative and policy-oriented and not merely confined to presentation of empirical findings' (Alternatives 1975 p.1). The significance for Peace Research is the infusion of extra impetus to normative and creative thinking, in addition to work done in the empiricist mode. The journal has been consistent in this in its three decades of publication and has cast its net widely to include articles from all parts of the globe.

What is notable about the journal 'International Interactions' is that it was established to act as a bridg e in light of emerging splits in Peace Research. Appearing first in 1974 as a transnational and interdisciplinary journal, it was 'to serve as a medium for publishing empirical studies and think pieces which cover a wide range of international interactions'. The journal sought, with the Peace Research movement in apparen t difficulties, to be cat holic in its interests and a bridge, 'between scholars of different styles' a statement that appears in each issue. For our purposes what is notable is the composition of the Editorial Advisory Board; edited by Edward Azar, the Board included Elise Boulding, Herbert Kelman, Anatol Rapoport, Bart Landheer, Dieter Senghaas and Michael Nicholson. Of their interests and emphases it could be said that they were wide-ranging.

It is interesting to note the journal 'Peace and Change,' for it too was a relative latecomer in the field, with a clear aim to explain its existence. It sought to invest Peace Research with an historical dimension and was, perhaps, also a response to the influence of empiricism in North America. Of this journal, Chatfield says that 'it has been the chief organ of the Conference on Peace Research in History and the C onsortium on Peace Research, Education and Development and it explicitly relates to constituencies beyond academia. Partly for this reason, it lacks a f irm basis of support and its future is problematical' (Chatfield 1979 p .165). In this, Chatfield was being rather pessimistic for the Consortium on Peace Research, Education and Development (COPRED) endured with a separate identity until, in 2001, it j oined together with the Peace Studies Association, to form the Peace and Justice Studies Association, with the stated aim of bringing 'together academics, teachers and grassroots activists to ex plore alternatives to violence and share visions and strategies for social justice and social change'. The first part of the Journal's twenty-eighth volume appeared in 2003.

If that comment from Chatfield is indicative of time, place and circumstance, then so too is that of Nicholas Onuf who, in 1975, suggested of American Peace Research that 'by deferring to established enterprises like world order studies and International Relations, Peace Research is denying itself an intelligible core. Work undertaken is collectively diffuse and individually undisciplined' (Onuf 1975 pp.71-2). Arguably, the core around which much of the work done in the United States coheres nowadays is a combination of world order studies, peace and justice studies and conflict resolution (with the Institute for Conflict Analysis and Resolution at Georg e Mason University , where John Burton was an early prime mover, a major presence). It is, now hard to sustain the view that is a degree of lack of discipline; 'anything goes' is not acceptable now, if it ever was. Indeed, there is a clear n etwork of interconnectedness, with scholars sharing similar aims and objectives, albeit with different strategies, but still researching peace in its many dimensions. A detailed survey of the journal literature is beyond our scope here, but is evident that a perennial theme, at the beginning and since, that a sense of individual and collective self-awareness has been the hallmark of Peace Research. How does it stand in relation to existing disciplines? What are its core concerns? Is it parochial? Where is it coming from and going to?

And yet, journals continue to appear. The 'International Journal of Peace Studies' appeared in 1996. 'The Journal of Peace Education' appeared in 2004. Perhaps this is indicative of a stage reached in the development of Peace Research and the question of Peace Research and 'peace thinking' (a wider term?) in the curriculum. We can assume that COPRED (given kits guiding principles and aims) has\been instrumental in the area of education in the United States; attendance at its conferences brings others into contact with like-minded professions actually teaching with a firm base in the undergraduate curriculum. But much remains to be done, needless to say.

Nevertheless, if the planned journal aimed a different audience with a slightly different set of objectives indicates anything, it may be that we have got that much nearer to the goal set out by David Singer in 1976, when he argued that 'Peace Education, widely conceived, may well turn out to be the most important activity of peace researchers. That is, even if we mount a major and successful research assault on the problems of war and social justice, of what value will it be if the rest of the world neither believes nor understands our discoveries, even assuming that some of the world's citizens hear about it? We must also write up our results in language that is clear, spell out some of our procedures in explicit and reproducible detail and examine the pragmatic implications carefully and imaginatively. In doing so, we not only contribute to the body of knowledge that may save us. We also increase the likelihood that that those who hear and must act on this knowledge will be able to understand what we have discovered, evaluate it critically and interpret it intelligently' (Singer 1976 p.9). Nobody ever pleaded for rigour in Peace Research than David Singer and he was surely informed that an agenda of Peace education should emerge from the work done over [then twenty, now] fifty years of concerted endeavour. In other words, there is sufficient work done, capable of interpretation and distillation in order that it be made intelligible. It would be informed by rigorous analysis, conceptual consistency allied to innovation and clearly relevant to an agenda of change. Thinking about change and wanting it and willing it badly will not be enough; evidence of what works, what does not work, what are self-defeating strategies informed by wrong assumptions and wrong mindsets, the accumulated costs of sticking to dysfunctional policies are important issues readily comprehensible and, perhaps, readily capable of informing an agenda of Peace Education. It is incontrovertibly the case, in the words of the eminent British scientist Sir Peter Medawar, that 'we know enough to be able to do better' (Medwar 1986). That may not exhaust the debate, but such debate as takes place must surely be better informed that was the case, say, twenty years ago.

Chapter 5

The Substantive Content of Peace Research: An Interpretation

As the subtitle of this work indicates, it is an interpretation of Peace Research. It is not intended as definitive, but rather instrumental, to stimulate engagement as to the relationship between participants in the endeavour and others; and to examine the relationships between Peace Research and International Relations on the other. From the perspective of the twenty-first century, this is how it seemed then and seems now.

This is not an exhaustive content analysis of journals, books and conference papers. Those who seek them now have unprecedented means to access them via the internet. Search-engines provide volumes of information and masses of potential links to related organizations, institutes and so on. Many organizations provide precise details of their earliest histories, with SIPRI being a prime example. There are now electronic journals. From invisible college, to visibility and on to cyberspace!

So where are we now? The past fifty years of Peace Research might be split into five phases. Firstly, the pioneers emerged with a critical stance. They found a voice, perhaps a small one at first, but they were not put off by the weight of the momentum against them. Again, it is worth pointing out that the pioneers of Peace Research took on the accumulated wisdom and knowledge of five thousand years and more. Fifty years, set against that, is no time at all, but it has been a productive five decades. Second, the early participants sought not only a degree of collectivity, but also the means to short-term survival and medium-term viability. The long-term might have seemed a little optimistic at that stage. Thirdly, having established a base of sorts, they sought to articulate and engage with a research agenda, both about substantive concerns and the nature, scope and limits of Peace Research itself; there has always been a code of self-reflection, rather than over-confidence and complacency. Fourth, there has been the accumulation of evidence, conceptual innovation and the creation of a new discourse of war, peace and conflict, much of it innovative insofar as it was rejectionist, finding loaded or misleading implications embodied in existing discourse. At the same time, there has been technical innovation, with regard to the interpretation of, intervention in and resolution of conflicts. These skills ought not to be underestimated, though they are not always evident – or are frequently taken for granted – even as conflicts are being resolved. Perhaps it is testimony to the roles of facilitators and third parties that the parties to the conflict shift to a new level of interaction, feeling that 'we did it ourselves'. And, as new vocabulary creeps in to general discourse, its origins and sources are hardly acknowledged. It is, for example, interesting to note how much of mainstream dialogue is informed by the notion of structural violence (in relation to development policies and, most obviously and most recently, in terms of the 'war on terror' and its root cau ses. Galtung is rarely, if ever, mentioned. Now, of course, we know that these things are as they are – though we did not see it that way then. Fifth, we are engaging with the promise of the new, taking Peace Research forward to e ngage with a wider agenda of multi-dimensioned peace and security agenda. This includes, inter alia, AIDS, water, the availability of drugs, the nature and nurture of the global environment, the interconnectedness of the ecosphere, the threat of pollution and allied issues. These are not part of the traditional agenda of security politics, nor were they high on the agenda of Peace Research in the early days. Yet there came a radical ch ange in social cosmology in the sixties for we saw ourselves for what we, the human race, are: a collectivity on a s mall ball spinning in space. We had never seen ourselves like this before, ever.

1.   The Question of Science

Insofar as Peace Research has sought to free itself from the traditionally systematic, but essentially, folk/literary approach to knowledge about questions of war, peace an d conflict it has been only partially successful. We have not yet begun to approach a body of knowledge that is a bona fide 'science of peace' the nomenclature and title o f the Walter Isard inspired 'Peace Science Society (International) notwithstanding. There has been much work of a systematic and scientific sort done. Insofar as science is concerned with a series of testable, tested and logically consistent set of statements that can be confirmed or disproved, then we have, in part, a body of knowledge that is 'scientific'. Moreover, it has a base in empirical evidence, systematically gathered rather than selected to fit an argument. There are s ignificant data-bases regarding the incidences of war and conflict. In other words, there have been some scientific discoveries which are n ot easily dismissed since they have an au thoritative status rooted in ev idence. In this they stand four-square consistent with the founding aims of Wri ght and Richardson: is assessing the causes of war and the conditions of peace, these followers have asked a series of questions that can be answered by reference to the evidence. Where? When? Duration? Casualties? Parties involved? And the like. At th e very minimum, such work exposes the selective blindness embodied in the conventional notions (they are there in the texts and the teaching) that the period 1815-1914 was a 'century of peace;' that, as Margaret Thatcher observed, by 1989 NA TO had ensured four decades of peace even as near to home hundreds were dying in Ireland; and , thirdly, sets in context discussions about the much-vaunted 'Long Peace.' Yes, we know what they mean in a restricted and not banal or vapid way, but it will simply not do to construct the conflict and peace question in these terms any longer. It is to disregard the evidence. In times of 'peace' (the absence of war for some) millions have died in violent conflicts. The absence of interstate war in a particular time and region is of no consequence to those being killed elsewhere.

There is, moreover, a body of work which, though not (always) grounded in an empiricist approach, is concerned with conceptual innovation regarding the explanations as to the causes, dynamics and consequences of war and conflict. This has its roots in observable human behaviour, rather in the validity of 'universalist' and essentialist propositions handed down from history. Furthermore, insofar as this literature reveals consistent patterns that pertain to all human conflicts, then there exists the basis for not only a generic approach to the study of conflict amongst human beings (at all levels of social complexity) but also the skeleton of a general approach to explaining human behaviour, rooted in behaviour, that is in terms of positivist, existential and actually-existing conditions that can be observed, experienced and captured by memory or i mages, and not in any normative and ethical traditional. In this sense, the work is positivist/behavioral, rather than prescriptive. This does not mean that any observations about ethics are superfluous, only that they are not always primary. In other words, we look at what people do when they behave and proceed to ex plain what it is that they do an d why. Explanation is the key here. Only by looking at the incidence of patterns of behaviour can we avoid the trap of assuming that norms exist (or ou ght to) and explain behaviour in terms of its (enforced/resisted) conformity with – or departure from – those norms. In the latter case, we get into issues of control and coercion that confuse the issue. For example, instead of insisting that schoolchildren should wear a uniform or a tie o f a minimum length, for this is what the rules dictate, we might ask whether and to what extent these are pri mary issues in reg ard to the learning process and the development of common values and good fellowship. The tie and the uniform might be a m eans to that end but the problem is that they interfere with the achievement of them since they are transformed into issue of 'discipline' and 'rules. Enforcement and sanctions are then resorted to.

Thirdly, a good deal of work done in the area of Peace Research has been formal, rigorous and heuristic. Not everyone has shared the enthusiasm for Game Theory and Theories of Bargaining, constituted as 'formal approaches' but proponents have seen value in this approach by virtue of its ab ility to follow through to a greater degree of complexity the consequences of interdepen dent decision-making in conditions of uncertainty. This allows a formal approach to the study of longer-term futures, insofar as this is consistent with the parameters of the game. A contrary view comes from Mary Clark, who points out the limitations of game theory and a key assumption of competitiveness. She argues that this calculated stress on selfishness is not implanted in our genes nor are ' pro-social behaviors a potential sacrifice. Such an assumption is arbitrary, depending on the observer's interpretation of the whole context of behavior. In fact the very idea of sacrifice in social behavior becomes quite unnecessary if all pos sible levels of natural selection are taken into account' (Clark 2003 p.72).

Likewise, with respect to questions of gaming and simulations. Gaming is essentially a series of role-playing 'games' where scenarios are pla yed out and patterns observed. These had their origins in the war games played in the military academies and staff colleges, but have since become generalized as a m eans to research and teaching. In this way, behaviour can be rep licated, analogies and homologies identified across systems and patterns established, as f or instance in the incidence of stress in decision-makers, the pressures of time, the operationalization of notions of crisis, the discernment of threats and the implications of such notions as 'groupthink' and 'tunnel vision'. All of this will draw on disciplines other than political science and international relations, to provide insights into the nature of human behaviour.

Similarly, we have put human behaviour into a wider context by looking at evolving areas of studies such as ecology and psycho-biology. In what respects is human behaviour comparable with other animals, principally the higher mammals and great apes? The findings here have been important in demonstrating recurrent patterns, with respect to the influences of territory, genetic endowment, hormonal distributions, collective security and spacing. Aggression is central to this agenda, more specifically when it i s manifest and when it i s sublimated. More recen t discoveries relating to the functioning of the brain have blurred distinctions between chemistry, physics, psychiatry and social psychology, by identifying the important role of chemical stimuli (more particularly their absence or presence) as these predispose personality types towards certain kinds of aggressive and violent behaviour. This raises again many of the issues associated with the questions of illness, deviance, confinement, imprisonment and illness not merely (or only) as medical questions but also regarding the power-related status of prevalent social norms. Society needs to be protected from some types of behaviour – for example as displayed by psychopaths – but discrimination remains a key issue, as between illness on the one hand and 'deviance' on the other (see Box 1971 and Foucault *ouevre*).

There is much to do, but of this work we can say that it has been consistent with the procedures of science; self-correcting, systematic, rooted in evidence and cumulative in the longer run. In recent decades the challenge to a uthority and power represented by the postmodernist challenge has thrown into sharp relief the question of foundationalism, (Fairlamb 1994), categories of discourse as categories of power/control and 'the canon'. The point is well taken, with respect to some, but not all, of the critical comments that have come from that perspective. But the baby should not be thrown out with the bathwater. In other words, we have some points of reference to s uggest, that is, that Beethoven and Rap are both authentic expressions of the conditions of being human in a given time and space; there is also reason to s uggest that we can discriminate as between one and the other, which does not suggest a hierarchy of taste, class, power or gender. There is still room for a t heory of aesthetics, even in a ti me of skepticism about the role of science and cynicism about art and power. Rap and Beethoven challenge our aesthetic frame of reference; they do not negate it; rather it is to raise q uestions with regard to its actualization in different circumstances.

To summarize, to aim to be scientific is not to be rooted in empiricism. But there is more to empiricism than seeking to adhere to the cult of the fact. At its worst, this gave rise to the idea associated with the grasping out for computers in the 1960s where the effects, at their very worst, were to establish that Uganda was poorer that California; GIGO = garbage in and garbage out. We needed to say more than the blindingly obvious.

So the critics who point out that Peace Research was empiricist miss the general point. Following Wright and Richardson in the search for evidence, an empiricist approach was necessary, desirable and consistent. But the search for evidence, as opposed to a location within metaphysics, was more than about simply counting things and classifying them. It was dater gathering via a variety of routes, with some of them being identified above. And, incidentally, as regards International Relations, behaviouralism in International Relations was directly traceable back to the initiatives of Lasswell and Merriam at Chicago, who sort to free thinking about politics from emphases on the structural, procedural and legal.

Empiricism is one aspect of scientific thinking which, above all, should be rigorous, critical and a process that unites scholars is the field: science is done by individuals, but always in a collectivity. This is why the journals matter as a medium, peer review of papers as a process and the conference and symposium as a means to wider dissemination and critique. Looking at the early journals, the emphasis on the empirical seems like a means to be taken seriously, to make the research look serious – becau se it was. It was not journalism, it was not impressionistic and it was not idiosyncratic. As such it demanded to be taken seriously. And over the years, it was. By 1969 (sic!) Peace Research was deemed 'respectable' (Pruitt and Snyder 1969 p.ix), with that comment followed by others to the effect that Peace Research was characterized by 'rigorous empirical enquiry' whereas work previously done was often 'overly simplistic.' Which it surely was.

And, as if to make the point about the partiality of the critics' perspective, whilst the empirical agenda was being addressed enthusiastically, others, hardly marginal, were pursuing other tasks associated with building the foundations, via the route of conceptual innovation and creative thinking.

2.   The Question of Reflexivity and Change

Apart from the question of methodology, of which a di scussion of empiricism is but one aspect, there is one other striking feature of P eace Research that is so obvious that it scarcel y gets the attention it s urely deserves. Attention to it was prompted by McSweeney's comment regarding an apparent lack of focus in Peace Research with the end of the Cold War. What is striking is that Peace Research as an enterprise and Peace Researchers as a co mmunity of scholars, have been remarkably self-aware and self-critical. There has been an astonishing process of introspection, self-and collective-examination. (Two examples will suffice here by way of indication. Galtung (1988) on the prospects for the next twenty-five years of Peace Research; Kaye (1987) on the 'hard questions.' The journals are replete with similar questions).

Again, looking at the work done is revealing. What were the aims and objectives of Peace Research? What were its priorities? How 'Radical' could it be? How 'Radical' should it be? What were its boundaries and responsibilities? What were the criteria of relevance? Were some lines of enquiry more or less important than others? Where are we now? What are our priorities for the next two decades? What does this new journal seek to do that the extant ones do not do? What is the utility of game theory? What was the role of Wright and Richardson? What progress have we made? What sort of work has come from which regions? If Peace Research was akin to being an 'applied science' how could this process of application be imagined, targeted and implemented? How did one wing the Peace Research movement relate to the other, where the whole was a collective enterprise, but consistent with individual stances? Was there an obligation to sign petitions or take part in p olitical demonstrations? Or produce relevant work, the value of which would demand attention?

There is clear ev idence of the existence of a proces s of critically engaged reflexive reconstruction, for as the context within which Peace Research sought to be relevant to changes taking place – rapidly, cumulatively and often confusingly – then stasis was never an option. Stasis in other field was deemed to part of the problem, as was the search for knowledge for its own sake. Peace Research sought to be relev ant to qu estions of war peace an d conflict. So, j ust as the verdict 'respectable' was being delivered in 1969, relative turmoil prevailed, in the context not only of the war in Vietnam, but wars elsewhere in the Third World. Was it the role of Peace Research to be an instrument of revolution? Was this consistent with the goal of being Radical? What was the relationship between Marxism and Peace Research?

It is, of course, hard to reconstruct this mood from our contemporary perspective. But it is there in the journals and papers to be engaged: it is a certain type of ephemera of lasting and didactic value and significance. And its significance should not be underestimated.

To take but two specific examples. In 1972, in a short paper of less than fifty typed pages addressed questions associated with: the relationships between knowledge and action; the applicability of findings; the relationship between Peace Research and the status quo; the question of bias; the relationships between morality and elites; moral dilemmas and empirical problems. He concluded that the debate about the future of Peace Research 'has made it increasingly clear t hat many of the comfortable beliefs (sic!) and assumptions which peace-oriented scholars have held regarding the purpose and impact of their work on the outside world may be outmoded or naïve' (Wallace 1972 p.48). Two years later, Michael Banks argued that we needed to c ome up against various problems 'of biased perception, the social position of the researcher and the moral consequences of interventions in conflict situations' (Banks 1974 p.36). In other words, we need to be constantly aware that as the field changes, then so ought we to feel the need to keep pace. Oth erwise we run th e risk of being rendered naïve. And if, informed with such knowledge as we have, we seek to intervene in conflicts, then we ought to be very careful about the implications of what we do: we might get people killed.

This does not exhaust the list of problems. It is not simply a question of the acquisition of academic skills: there is also the question of stance. What are we to do? What are we teach – a nd how do we define, respect and adhere to t he distinction that separates education from political indoctrination. Be sure that if we do not constantly see it clearly, others will look for it, and the transgressions. And so they did.

This is in no way to suggest that there was a test of conscience involved by way of an engagement with Peace Research. Surely, all were committed in some degree, otherwise they would have gone and done something simpler: politics, direct action, alternative lifestyle or ornithology? Yet it is to suggest that engagement and involvement meant a necessary and consequent addressing of certain questions and, having addressed these, it is hard to feel that people would assume that, having gained admission, as it were, they could then coast. Involvement means constant awareness: being 'involved' means that ornithology is not enough. We are talking here about a life-stance, not a hobby.

Probably some (could we ever know how many?) did assume that once a big decision was confronted, they were in. But for the individual and the collectivity, Peace Research is a question of constant self-awareness. And the consistent, persistent and open-ended quest demonstrates that questions were being asked that could never be answered definitively. Relevance depends on context. Action depends on opportunities. Teaching opportunities depend upon institutional initiatives as well as personal agendas. The point is that the point of the process is change and adaptation. We never 'get there:' we do not seek a desired end state, for we know that peace is not a condition of stasis, but emancipation and adaptation. Peace is process, not Utopia.

If we assume, not unreasonably, that the problems of war, peace and conflict have not been ameliorated (which does not, in itself, render the signal achievements of Peace Research a 'waste of time' or futile or peripheral), and a reference to context is significant here, then the questions thus far addressed in this section have not got any easier to answer for subsequent generations of scholars. In other words, we have an agenda of choice, relevance, stance and so on in contemporary circumstances, where the agenda has become infinitely more complicated. It is not simply a question of the avoidance of (nuclear) war – if that ever was a simple question. It never was; it was pressing, all-consuming and very, very hard, such were the dangers. We were frightened. It is a question, now, of addressing an agenda of both absence and presence: the absence of conditions that make for destructive conflict and the presence of conditions that make for positive peace, at all levels of human interaction: from the intra-personal, to the global, no less.

There is a new agenda, since we have adapted over five decades. But the point is that Peace Research has adapted to, and defined, this changing agenda. It is hard to see how one could come to the conclusion that, at the end of the Cold War, Peace Research was, somehow, 'stuck for something to do.' All we need to do is to paraphrase and bastardize Sir Christopher Wren: if you seek an agenda, look about you. It had constructed an agenda of structural violence, material deprivation and marginalization; violence and oppression, not to mention questions of ethnic identity and the status of indigenous peoples. By the time we got to the end of the Cold War, consistent with the innovations associated with the developed Peace Research agenda, that which was hidden to most was revealed to more.

To reiterate: these questions did not disappear in 1989, nor did they suddenly appear. There was an agenda to engage with, not an agenda to create. Many knew that they were there all along: look in the journals of Peace Research for a Feminist agenda – its presence there being a res ponse to a dev eloped Feminist agenda. Cynthia Enloe was working on aspects of gender and feminism at the Richardson Institute for Conflict and Peace Research in London in 1972! Without the works of Germaine Greer, Betty Freidan, Sheila Rowbotham and Gloria Steinem, nothing that came later would have been possible: they started the process of visibility. As Shiela Rowbotham put it, before the 1970s, women were 'hidden from history.' They were there as it ev olved, they played their part – a s did th e men and the children, but they had no place. T he English labour historian Edward Thompson revealed the part played in economic development by the 'English working class' who were likewise hidden from history; he sought to rescue them from oblivion (Thompson 1968) – and then went on to becom e a peace activ ist of great significance.

To conclude, if Peace Research has not been responsive, adaptive and receptive of inputs from elsewhere, it has been nothing. It could never avoid a stance of self-consciousness, and be con sistent with its defining impulse. That it has is entirely the point; if relevance is the guiding watchword, then adaptation is the life-blood of the enterprise. What acts as focus, goal and binding-force is the dynamic conception of peace, constituted by both absence and presence, negative and positive components. The centre of the project/endeavour is the problem: the problem moves on, with changed circumstances. Rather glibly (or thankfully), but not entirely inappropriately, we might cite, Cynthia Kerman's notion of 'creative tension' (which she related to Kenneth Boulding's work), that binds together the purpose, method and dynamics of Peace Research. Without it, the whole thing falls apart.

3.   The Question of Armaments

A focus on armaments is a central element of the Peace Research agenda. It is also indicative of relative degrees of emphasis associated with perspective. Certainly, it is a key element of the 'sharp-end' and policy-relevant agenda of Peace Research. So, too, is it a k ey element in the policy agenda of International Relations and Strategic Studies, so we need to be rather more subtle in addressing this key issue. The idea of the arms trade and the 'merchants of death' has a lo ng history, predating the First World War and the League. There were those of a liberal persuasion who took the view that all o f this was inimical to the achievement of peace and prosperity. Though the Nineteenth-century advocates of Free Trade (and precursors of the later notion of 'Functional Cooperation) assumed that this would be beneficial, and war would interrupt the production of benefits. There existed an alternative view.

The notion of the 'Balance of Power' carried with it also the idea the of means to balance. More of this could be used to balance more of the that, not only in this state, but also in terms of allies. In this view, arms transfers and 'arms races' need not, always, be con strued as inimical to in ternational security. Indeed, arms transfers and stable arms dynamics might be means to 'stable peace' and stable deterrence.' If the risk of instability meant increasing the risk of war, then a means of stability must be found. Stability was a central element of 'Grand Strategy,' be this numbers, tonnage, limits or ratios.

So, within a ' conventional' frame of reference, as it were, (where conventional does not connote non-nuclear weapons, but established ways of thinking), more weapons could be construed as better, a means to stability and a means to 'peace.' The study of weapons acquisition was thus a legitimate object of research, for both students of Peace Research and Strategic Studies. For the latter, it was part of a study of the conditions necessary for stable (nuclear) deterrence, in terms of both central strategic deterrence and extended deterrence; in other words the defence of allies. It was a legitimate means to an end, and a desirable end at that, given the alternative of an unstable transition into nuclear war.

For the former, however, consistent with the established notion that the 'merchants of death' were part of the problem and that 'more means worse,' armaments constituted more of a problem. Arms transfers led to regional tensions and instabilities, increased the risks of war and cumulative problems. Ample testimony exists by reference to the arms supply policies of the United States and Soviet Union to client states in the Middle East.

Yet the Cold War gave rise to an agenda, and a community, associated with the question of 'arms control' where the question was not one of disarmament, with which the critics of the 'merchants of death' would surely have agreed. On the contrary, arms control was concerned with the perverse notion of collaboration between adversaries, with regard to arm aments, and indeed cooperation in their proliferation. However, cooperation in proliferation might also mean building up to agreed limits. And so it was that, in the 1970s, the United States and the Soviet Union agreed a Strategic Arms Limitation Treaty in 1972 that set numerical limits and allowed (or, in terms of the critics, stimulated) the building up to these limits.

This is not the place for an extended discourse on the nature of arms control and strategic interaction. Nevertheless, it is an appropriate place to c ompare and contrast assumptions. For the Strategists, for whom arms control was deemed part of the agenda of strategic interaction, this was all le gitimate: more could mean stability. More weapons were a means to an end, not necessarily worse. For the Peace Researchers, these beliefs were perverse in their foundations and even more so in their consequences. How could more mean better? How could arms proliferation mean stability (a question which, incidentally, had preoccupied the 'formal' game theorists within Peace Research, who sought to establish the nature and dynamics of stability conditions associated with the perennial problems of arms races)?

For the Strategists, arms were a means to an end and not always a problem in themselves, though they sometimes could be. For most Peace Researchers, more meant worse. Therein lies an indication of the different emphases as between the International Institute of Strategic Studies at o ne end of the spectrum and the Stockholm International Peace Research Institute at the other. Each approached the question from different ends of the spectrum: and each was differently funded in consequence. Both sought to be relevant, accurate, contemporary in their accumulation of data, from appropriate sources. Each s ought to be auth oritative, given that it was beyond the capabilities or credibility of governments to seek, directly, the military capabilities of potential adversaries. Each became authoritative. The different emphases may be explained in these terms: for SIPRI, arms were part of the problem. For the IISS, they were often part of the problem; but sometimes they were part of the solution, where the solution is discussed in terms of stability, management, control and limitation. SIPRI had, and has, a different agenda, which is why one is an institute concerned with Strategic Studies and one is concerned with an agenda of Peace Research. The telescope has two ends and two perspectives.

The idea of 'arms as problem' has spilled over, to a wider question, beyond supply, demand and proliferation, to explore the questions of costs, opportunity costs and effects. With regard to the first, this is often couched in terms of the 'burden of armaments' where this is cast in terms on the various effects upon distortions of economies (in both producers and recipients), the implications for research and development and the consequences for the 'civil sector,' allied to the wider agenda associated with sectoral and industrial transformation associated with the conversion from defence- to civilian-related production (see, by way of example, Southwood 1991). With regard to the issues of opportunity costs, this has frequently been exemplified by reference to the impact of arms acquisition on recipients, especially where there are major questions associated with economic and welfare agenda considerations. Interestingly, newly independent countries sought the attributes of statehood, since they followed the logic of statehood: states had armed forces and a territory to protect. But they also had an agenda of economic development. One militated against the other and questions of development, consequently, spilled over into considerations of aid, inducements and corruption. What, precisely, were the causal connections between full arsenals on the one hand and empty stomachs on the other? And what was the connection between war and poverty in, for example, Africa? In other words, what was the impact of war and weapons on other aspects of life – or death? The environmental impact of weapons on the environment was a significant, and early, research project addressed by SIPRI, along with important questions relating to the arms race at sea, the proliferation of weapons, the militarization of space and impact of nuclear testing (details of these are available on the SIPRI website: relevant authors are Arthur Westing, Ian Anthony and Bupendra Jahsani, amongst others).

In this, SIPRI has been consistent with one of the founding principles of Peace Research; that it be problem centric and concerned with a policy agenda. SIPRI has not been alone in this task: for another example the Department of Peace Studies at Bradford University has also frequently put out critical reports on policy matters, such as arms control, defence budgets and arms transfers, relating to the performance of the British government, but not only it (Owen Greene and Malcolm Chalmers have been major contributors, and they have acted as witnesses to the House of Commons Defence Committee frequently, surely significant in itself, and for what it represents).

4.   The Question of Conflict

The traditional dichotomy as between domestic politics on the one hand and international politics on the other, the one being the preserve of domestic authorities and 'good government,' the other addressing the problem of order in a potentially chaotic world, gave rise to a rather limited set of perspectives on the nature of conflict.

In the domestic sphere, conflict was often dealt with in terms of questions of deference, respect for law and order, conformity and the like. To take one example: the classic text of (American?) sociology in the 1950s was 'The Social System' by Talcott Parsons (Parsons 1951). The task, in effect, was to explain how a pluralist society, such as the United States was then perceived to be, could and should work. All would have a voice and a say, some would win and some would lose but, in the end, all would get something and the stable system would reproduce itself, stable and satisfying, for most of the people and for most of the time. With one set of qualifications: a good many lost a lot of the time, even most of the time. In other words, conflict was almost entirely lost from the conventional, even dominant, analyses of society. Where there was disorder, then authority would be exercised, the law resorted to and punishment inflicted. The power of social norms was said to be significant. Subcultures – of race, gender and identity – were, by and large, invisible. There were very many good reasons why Ralph Ellison gave the title 'Invisible Man' to his novel that dealt with the Black experience in post-war America (Ellison 1952). Conformity and discipline were remarkable in terms of their effects: hair would be short, skirts would be long, sex was within marriage – which was for life – and divorce was disgrace. Children would respect their elders and betters; they would seldom be heard – but they were often hurt, one way or another. And so were women.

Civil order was the agenda of internal government, through a system of arrangements. In international affairs, conflict was amenable to treatment by methods subsumed under the rubric of 'diplomacy' and where it was not so resolved , then war was deemed to the means of last resort. This all seems so sensible – except that it all, now, looks so limited in terms of perspective and perhaps even primitive in terms of underlying assumptions. Societies were rife with conflict: according to issues of race, class, gender and the like. But 'order' seemed never to be perceived in   such terms. 'Rioters' were shot (the Paris Commune of 1871 being but one example) or imprisoned (the British Miners' Strike of 1984 another). Minorities were repressed, by one means or another. To take but one example: Duke Ellington's band may have entertained white audiences in plush hotels with their 'big-band jazz' – but that had to leave after the performance and stay 'black' hotels elsewhere. And Sam Cooke was still, in the 1960s, singing that 'A Change is Gonna Come' – and so it did. And it needed to be explained. Was it to do with the power of non-violence? The example of Ghandi? 'People Power?' 'Black Power?' The new-found effects and 'power' of television?

The point is simply this: war received attention; how could it not? But conflict seemed not to be an issue at all. Societies worked, more or less: the law worked, more or less: life moved on, more or less – for less rather than more. And sometimes wars came along, increasingly for more, rather than for less.

Then we discovered that conflict was a major issue in terms of the functioning of societies, across the globe. We discovered, or were made to discover, that concealment, incarceration and coercion were unproductive strategies. Spaces opened up, to allow differences to be made manifest (the end of conscription in Britain?). Resistance made a space to allow difference to be made visible (France and Algeria – which allowed us to engage with the work of Franz Fanon). Revolt demanded attention in the United States – as recently as the 1960s. In summary, conflict demanded attention. And it got it as the contents of the first Peace Research journals demonstrate. They were not unique in this, for the issues were too big to miss; but they were, with others, instrumental.

The early journals in Peace Research soon went beyond the limits of Parsonian analysis. And they also went beyond the assumptions that underpinned the functioning of advanced Western liberal de mocracies. In that, they were expansive and unconventional.

In general terms, with regard to the question of the nature of conflict, we can construct a trip artite system. First, th ere is th e notion that conflict has origins, based on the fundamental premise that it is n ot a 'given' associated with original sin, human nature or similar notions. Second, there is the issue of conflict dynamics. Why do some conflicts get better, some get worse and some get violent? These various dynamics and consequences need to be ex plained, when conventional explanations – associated with coercion, control and collapse and conformity – simply will not do. Thirdly, there is t he question of conflict termination: why do some conflicts, quite simply, not end? Why are some conflicts more persistent than others? Why is it that we have had wars in the Middle East in 1948, 1956, 1967, 1973 and since? Bad luck? 'Lack of will' (whatever that might mean)? Why did it tak e the British over three decades to get to grips with the conflict in the north of Ireland? In retrospect, we can say, in light of the work done in the last five decades, that these questions were little understood, at least in terms of the conventional assumptions and methods (e.g. 'we will not negotiate with terrorists'. But if you do not negotiate with terrorists, who influence events, with whom will you negotiate?) If the conventional methods did not apply, it seemed, quite simply, that they were not being applied appropriately or i mplemented enough: so the remedy seemed clear.

Now we do know more. We know about the origins of conflict. In terms of socialization, perception (a hugely important issue, and key agenda item in terms of the Cold War constructions of 'otherness'), wrong assumptions, stress, f ear, structures of behaviour and socialization, to name but a few relevant features. By way of example, take the case of the north of Ireland. 'Difference' lead to separation and separation lead to different patterns of interactions and socio-political/religious constructions of the images of the other. Forget that one community rarely had anything to say to, or do with, the other. All that they need to know, they knew and the facts would not get in the way. It was the same with the Americans and the Soviet Union in the Cold War: construction was all, encounter counted for nothing at all. Structures of engagement and images seemed to be self-reproducing.

So, structure and perception were constituent elements in the evolving elements of the frame of reference. But this was but the beginning. Origins of conflict in particular and human behaviour in general were to be sought beyond conventional limits of structure and process. Why, as human being – and not just as political animals/beings – did we do what we did? Were there other frames of reference that might be engaged? In summary, yes – and they were. The causes of conflict were to be found by reference to the agenda of psychology, sociology, anthropology, animal behaviour and the like. Politics had a role to play, but it was not always primary. Genes, group dynamics, socialization, education, culture, gender and the like were all relevant: no perspective seemed to have a prior call; much was to be researched and discovered. Did children follow the examples of parents, or peers or television images? Did they copy images of violent behaviour? For how much violence in society were the cartoon characters Tom and Jerry or the Roadrunner responsible, it any at all? Did children witness characters being squashed, bashed, run-over and blown-up with harmful consequences for themselves or others? Did children really copy what they had seen on television? Did adolescents and adults? Sometimes they did, the evidence suggested. Could they learn to be cooperative in appropriate settings and nurturing situations? What, precisely, was the relationship between 'nature' and 'nurture?' How could the effects of one be measured, set against the other? Few of these questions have been answered to the satisfaction of all. That they crop up in popular discussions in the various media so frequently is entirely the point: old assertions will no longer suffice. Much remains to be done. Peace Researchers have not said all that can be said. Asking the question 'what causes conflicts in human societies' demands serious examination of existing structures and processes where conflicts seem to be endemic.

But once a conflict is, so to say, in being, why do some conflicts take one form and why do others take another? Why do some conflicts persist, 'stumble along' and some get more and more violent? There is no resort or comfort here in the notion that what will be will be. There is a stark agenda: not of the origins of conflict, but the dynamics of conflicts. What, in short, is the problem? The problem is that dynamics of conflict are, even yet, little understood, relatively speaking. Progress has been, of that there can be little doubt. The efforts that have emanated from Peace Research have been significant but not, yet, decisive, in terms of facilitating or prompting a step-level change in assumptions, widely shared. Too many current practices are deeply-rooted in conservative assumptions, from the treatment of children and adolescents and the responses to crime. On the positive side, we can say that there is a body of research that can be engaged fruitfully in a time of difficulty.

With regard to the consequences of conflict, there is still an open-ended agenda. Where a conflict is not 'resolved,' what are the options? If there is a peace to be kept, in terms of an agenda of peacekeeping, what kind of peace is to be kept? By whom? Where? When? For, and/or on behalf of whom? At what cost? Borne by whom? To what purpose – in the immediate, short, medium and long term? And if there is a 'term' beyond the medium or long, is this a symptom of failure? The experiences of the former Yugoslavia may be in structive in this regard. What 'peacekeeping' means and, more importantly, what it means, in terms of an agenda of choice, instrumentalities and 'peaceful resolution' sets, in fact, another agenda. If a 'peace' is to be k ept, what does this mean? Separation? Interposition? Policing?

Finally, the functions of conflict demands attention, for the research shows that it can have positive functions in certain circumstances. Of Kenneth Boulding's view of conflict, Cynthia Kerman has this to say: 'It may surprise some who think of Boulding as a peacenik to learn that his ideal is actually a "perpetual state of unresolved conflict"; that he believes "Conflict is essential to any form of progress." Conflict is creative; evolution and learning could not have taken place without it' (Kerman 1974 p.266). In other words, the problem is not conflict in the abstract, but conflict in terms of consequences for those involved, directly or otherwise.

5.   The Question of Conflict Resolution

Traditional approaches to conflict resolution have actually amounted to a contradiction in terms. Conflicts have been settled, but resolved infrequently. Negotiation strategies have been developed that have been thought to be ' hard-nosed' and contrived to show resolve. Thus, trade unions and employers have negotiated about pay, with one demanding 10% as a rise, the other offering 2.5% and both settling for 5%. Each is 'h appy' with the settlement, but would have preferred a different outcome: they can 'live with it' or 'sell it to their members'. If there is a stalemate in the direct negotiations, then they can (or may be required to) take the case to arbitration, binding or otherwise. They may not wish to speak directly one to the other, but instead use the 'good offices' of a 'third party'.

This is well known as a co nventional approach. But it does not amount to conflict resolution. Nor may it deal with the underlying causes of the conflict, or the main issue. Resolution changes the basis of the relationship; if you will, the issue that divides the parties 'goes away' and ceases to be an   issues in their relationship. Settlement tends to leave residual issues un-discussed, perhaps undisclosed, so that the relationship, though it improves in some measure, remains unaltered in its structure and its   behavioural content and consequences. The opposition to the Good Friday Agreement in Ireland on the part of the Democratic Unionist Party (led by Ian Paisley) led to constant conflicts with the Ulster Unionist Party and, ultimately, the electoral success of the Paisley faction in the elections to the Ulster Assembly in the autumn of 2003. T he Good Friday Agreement is therefore controversial one more and the Assembly remains suspended, with the province ruled from London. And all of this years after the Agreement was signed. Yet the conflict remained – an d remains – un resolved. There are still issues that are not addressed or incapable of being addressed.

Moreover, that which is the ostensible cause of the conflict may be but a superficial issue. Pay is often an issue as between workers and management.

However, disputes about pay may be the means to express frustrations on the part of workers who are told what to do, as opposed to being asked; treated as ciphers rather than human beings; and, often, told to be grateful that they have a job when they would appreciate a degree of recognition for work done by being thanked. In other words, often the traditional approaches to disputes miss the point. What is at issue in the conflict? Who are parties to it? What are the symptoms and what are the causes? Again, to take a relevant example. As the negotiations took place in Paris to terminate the war in Vietnam, much debate was devoted to the shape of the table; cartoonists rather sardonically suggested coffin shapes. The real issue was not the shape of the table: rather, it was about who was to sit at it and who was to negotiate for whom. The parties to a conflict and its resolution do not need to have attained legal status: they have a behavioural status by virtue of their having a role to play in the conflict and a stake in its behavioral outcomes. The British detained Jomo Kenyatta and, later, Archbishop Makarios: both were said to be terrorists with whom the British would not negotiate. Both were freed from detention, played a part in the negotiations that saw Kenya and Cyprus achieve independence from the British and their assumption of the role of President of their newly-independent states. More recently, Gerry Adams and Martin McGuiness in Ireland have, necessarily, emerged as key actors in the Ireland peace process, having previously been marginalized and detained. There are numerous other examples that might be cited here to validate the point at issue: it is simply stated; what, ultimately, is this conflict about – and to whom does it matter. The answers to those questions are fundamental to the resolution process.

Cumulative research has illuminated the role of third parties, beyond the agenda of arbitration, judicial settlement and conventional approaches to bargaining, such as 'splitting the difference.' Third parties can be active or passive; they may be in contact with official or unofficial representatives of the parties to the conflict; they may act merely as a simple conduit, allowing each side to talk where communication hade become impossible (as in the case of husband and wife involved with a marriage in difficulties). At its simplest, the role of the third party may be simply to provide a means, and a non-interventionist means at that, to allow dialogue to take place. Again, we can ask the central question: how doe we engage the others if we do not engage them? Usually, we do so on the basis of history, belief or fear. Burton (1969) made major breakthroughs with an approach he early associated with 'conflict and communication'. Later this gave rise to an agenda of interactive conflict resolution. All of this was a long way from the other traditional practice of bringing the wisdom and experience of eminent and learned men to a conflict (as in the case of the Owen-Vance plan in the former Yugoslavia) to assist with their good offices. The accumulated research may be consulted through a variety of treatments, such as those from Mitchell and Banks (1996), Miall, Ramsbotham and Woodhouse (1999), Sandole and van der Merwe (1993), Fisher (1997), Dukes (1996), Tidwell (1998) and Vasquez et al (1995); there is certainly not a dearth of material. There may, however, still an agenda associated with changing practices.

Much of this literature aimed at conflict resolution throws into sharp relief the limitations of traditional approaches, not just to trade-union and employer relations, but also issues associated with arbitration and the like. More generally, it has the effect of raising serious questions about the very foundations of many political, social and legal systems that are b ased on opposition and adversarial relationships. Take, for example, the British legal system, which has been influential across the globe. The system is adversarial rather than inquisitorial. A jury is installed, evidence is presented and witnesses called. A verdict is reached and the accused is i nnocent or guilty. Yet t he system is devoted to getting an outcome, not solving the problem, as is e videnced by the number of controversial cases where persons have been found guilty, only to have the verdict overturned at appeal, sometimes after decades of incarceration. The insurance industry is frequently required to prove fault, liability or negligence in case o f accident, usually leading to lengthy court battles and huge legal costs, in turn spawning growth in the number of firms whose ethic is 'no win, no fee'. But we might ask where all o f this is leading? What happens when we get, ultimately and irrevocably, into a ' culture of complaint'? (Hughes 1993). Wh ere is the line between autonomy and integrity of self and the shift of 'blame' onto others? What is the ultimate end-state of this kind of society? Is it to be built on fault, blame and complaint as dominant social norms?

What of the question of 'no fault' procedures, where there is an acceptance of mutual liability? Where costs are kept to a minimum and, with them, social disruption is minimized. Clearly, this is unlikely to act in all ca ses: some employers are careless in relation to health and safety issues and some employees will not heed advice or act careles sly. In these sorts of cases, fault is a consideration and compensation important as part of the resolution of he case in law. But it may not be appropriate to assume that this is the norm. In the longer term we might also involve ourselves in a discussion as ton whether or not the law is only a means available to the wealthy and powerful and beyond the rest on grounds of cost alone. What, then, for the legal order when it is partial in terms of both access and outcomes? What remedies are available to the weak and poor?

In terms of adversarial relations, politics can be construed as a costly game, where procedures dictate or demand certain outcomes. It is the duty of Oppositions to oppose. So, is sue by issue, they criticize, pers onalize, demonize and ridicule their opponents. This, despite the fact that they have followed similar policies in the past and will adopt them in the future; different roles demand that difference be made manifest. They claim different specifics and changed circumstances, but the name of the game of debate is opposition, for the sake of oppos ition and in the nature of adversarial politics. Electoral systems that rely on the 'first past the post' system are s uspect, since a representative can be (an d often is) elected with significantly less than half of the total votes cast. First of all, they have to 'beat' the opposition.

This framework of assumptions is taken, by and large, to be the norm and is fostered in, for example, schools. There is rivalry in competitive sports, rivalry in intra-school competitions and, for example, in debating classes and societies. Parents encourage their children to be competitive. University degrees are awarded by class in Britain and a grade point average in the United States. There is thus an endemic stress associated with the need to succeed; a car, bicycle, computer or sweater may be the prize for success. Suicide is, for some, the tariff for failure.

This leads many to the view that competition is the normal order of things and that to be competitive is to win and be successful. This in turn leads to the consequential view that competition – and then conflict – can only be constructed in terms of winning and losing; alternative strategies of resolution are ruled out. Hence, 'good fences make good neighbours'.

After a while this presumed norm becomes no less than a social pathology. 'People need interactive communities, and the physical layout of their surroundings is a major prerequisite...The contemporary West's national "confrontational politics" needs to be replaced by collaborative problem-solving, focused on the local community, if environments and societies are to be restored to health' (Clark 2003 p.395).

In summary, whilst traditional, entrenched and conservative structures and processes are adhered to, conflicts persist (and are often fostered) and the consequences are left to pile up. Why? Because, to use a phrase that came to the fore with many of psychological studies associated with the Peace Research agenda, there is a wrong definition of the situation – which leads to wrong policies and, where these fail, resort to more of the same. Whatever else it is, conflict resolution is, simultaneously, an approach that can operate at all levels of conflict as well as constituting a decisive instrument of social change, adaptation and emancipation.

6.   Questions of Peace

For centuries, those who have sought peace have been derided; well-intentioned, but flying in the face of 'reality.' Five decades of research reveal not only the nature of conflict, conflict resolution strategies and techniques, but also key elements central to the construction of a radical new ontology of peace.

Disaffection with the structures and processes operational at all levels of society (and, compared to forty years ago, when we tended to assume that politics waas about parties and representation, whereas now we talk about the politics of self, family, church, group and various other collectivities) lead to a serious engagement with the tasks not only of conceptual innovation, but the development of a new consequent discourse of peace and conflict. Frequently derided as 'psycho-babble' and useless neologism, the new discourse (in a way similar to the recent innovations in Critical Security Studies) was frequently misunderstood where it was engaged at all. So mehow they did not seem to engage with the realities of the situation, it was said. Yet the principal point to make is that what was being said did actually confront – and explain – the realities of the situation, but in new ways, and the seminal contributions of Johan Galtung, John Burton and Kenneth Boulding are particularly instructive. Interestingly, all of these individuals have sought to be unconstrained by traditional academic boundaries and assumptions. Burton was trained in psychology, worked in the Australian Public Service, taught International Relations and was a prime mover in the development of Peace Research (see Dunn 2004, for a fuller treatment). Galtung was born in Norway, became a co nscientious objector, then a sociologist and specialist in methodological questions before, like Burton, playing a key role in Peace Research (see Lawler 1995 and Kruzel and Rosenau 1989 for fuller treatments). Boulding was born in Liverpool, educated at Oxford and left for the United States after graduation, to teach economics. Yet he too could not sit happily within the confines of economics, even though he wrote major texts (see K erman 1974 for a fuller treatment).

The volume of work that has come from these individuals is astonishing and it is not appropriate the try to précis it here, nor is that task central to our purpose here. What is central is to recognize the singular achievement of each – and all collectively – in the creation of new ways of thinking in light of their analysis and, yes, consequent diagnosis of the faults of the...no, not 'the old' but actually existing and reproducing systems of thought and behaviour Thus, each individual has provided the means to effect a breakthrough in the re-investment of 'peace' as a process of human emancipation and self-actualization.

For Burton, the key concept is 'provention' which he contrasts with traditional notions of prevention. Whilst the latter is limiting, the former is adaptive and expansive. Central to the idea of provention is Burton's notion that contemporary structures and processes do not enable fundamental human needs to be satisfied, indeed positively militate against their being satisfied. Need are not to be confused with wants. Fundamental human needs are associated with identity, authenticity, recognition and the like, as well as material needs, for food, shelter and so on. Insofar as needs are not satisfied, people will, ultimately, seek means to change the system where satisfaction is denied. It may be emigration, demands for change and, most problematic of all, violent conflict.

Constant themes in Boulding's prodigious output are the dynamics of human systems, the reolution of conflict consistent with variety and difference between and amongst human systems, all consistent with the process of human betterment. Constantly he urges us to change images, change social dynamics, develop a sense of time allied to future, to a stable peace that is also a dynamic peace, not a peace of stasis. Why? So that the prospects oh human betterment might be enhanced and the lot of humankind improved. With Burton, he is at o ne: we live in an unstable and un-peaceful world, but one where change is not only necessary and desirable, but possible.

This resonates with Galtung's fundamental contribution – the notion of structural violence. In fact, the implications of this idea have tended to s eep into common discourse over the years, not universal, but significantly so. The idea is simply explained and exemplified. Whereas 'violence' usually connotes the infliction of pain, injury and suffering through direct threat or action, the idea of structural violence suggests that people are being damaged in consequence of their actually existing conditions of life, which are damaging, limited and painful. Thus, there can be no such thing as a h appy slave or a p retty prison cell; th e one is incompatible with the other. What matters here is t he dominant and causative effects of structures.

We need not be surprised to find that Galtung's notion of structural violence has become common currency in the continuing discussions relating to economic development and the growing gap between rich and poor. Much of the debate has internalized Galtung's notion, working within the framework of its presumptions, if not recognizing it explicitly.

Galtung's emphasis on structure (in this part of his work at least) has a strong affinity with another signifiacant approach to the explanation of global dynamics that significantly challenges conventional assumptions. This has raised questions about the dynamics of the global system and its very origins. Traditionally, 1648 has been treated as the point of transition into a recognizably modern system of states. However, an emphasis on the transition into capitalism stresses an alternative dynamic. Associated with the work of Immanuel Wallerstein (1979a and 1979b, 1983 and 1984) and Andre Gunder Frank (1978, 1981), the approach termed 'World System Theory' comes out of a l iterature that shows a significant Marxist influence. Recall that, in the 1960s, studies of Marx experienced something of a renaissance; the Grundrisse (a forerunner of Das Kapital had been discovered and translated into English), the New Left was resurgent in North America and Europe and the bases of the social order were being brought into question. Nowhere was this more apparent than in the questioning of neo-colonialism and neo-imperialism. De-colonization had taken its course, but it was illusory and its consequences disastrous for the poor.

The valid picture, according to the adherents to a critical perspective, was not a world of states, equal and interacting, but unequal and existing in a condition of domination of the rich by the poor. The rich controlled from the centre, the poor existed at t he periphery and th e semi-peripheral states ensured that (in both exploiting and being exploited) the system persisted in a ten se fashion, without confronting the inherent dialectical oppositions in the system. All of this was due to the dynamics of modes of production (clearly drawn from Marx) so that antiquity gave way to feudalism, feudalism gave way to absolutism and this, in turn, gave way to capitalism. The modern world system was thus to be characterized as a dynamic of late capitalism where exploitation was operating on a global scale. In so operating, the exploitative dominance of capitalism was exploiting resources (land, labour and indigenous capital) and repatriating profits to the centre, the key cities at the heart of the capitalist nexus. The very system, in effect, was based on structural violence; low wages were paid, trade u nions opposed where they were not disallowed or pros cribed, workers coerced an d dismissed if they transgressed, to be replaced by others where there was seemingly endless pool of labour.

This might have been defended as spreading wealth on a g lobal scale, perhaps even a mode of economic development. Yet in many respects the improvements brought about – in terms of health, wealth, social cohesion and the like – were thought to be marginal at best. Millions still lived in shacks, surrounded by disease, subject to m arket forces where they relied on cas h crops and at t he mercy of weather and climate in vu lnerable areas. The problem was systemic, based on the accumulation of capital in the West, its shifting to poorer states in the form of loans and consequent patterns of default. This might have been the prelude to violent conflict in certain quarters (in face of corruption or shares of wealth going to preferred groups, consistent with clan, tribalism or cronyism), but it certainly amounted to s tructural violence. The life-chances of millions were minimized rather than enhanced and there can surely be no more dramatic depiction of the relevant processes, and their effects, than those represented in the portfolios of the contemporary photographers Sebasteao Salgado and James Nachtwey.

Clearly, there is a te nsion here with regard to what authorities regard as 'peaceful' relations and what the Peace Research literature, and other media, reveal. Authorities are the prisoners of system, role and time. They have agendas set by organizational requirements (such as getting elected) and time-frames that are by definition short term. Any academic who has involved policy-makers is struck by the time dimension; we, they say, have the luxury of the long view. But peace has a time dimension too and the long-term accumulated consequences of short term decisions taken as being consistent with 'pressing needs' (the profits of the firm or the health of the world economy?) are deleterious and harmful. We live in an un-peaceful world, but it may not look like this to relevant authorities. In their own terms, they may be con vinced that they are doing a g ood job. Incontrovertibly, the lot of many on the planet is bad. More to the point, it is not getting better, but worse. Needs are n ot being satisfied, betterment is illusory, violent structures persist.

This throws into sharp relief the tension between symptoms and causes. More often than not, authorities focus on symptoms. So, crime, migration, the collapse of values, decline in respect for authority and the like hold the centre stage. In the British General Election of 2005 ' respect' and how to somehow reclaim it was on the agenda. So, too, was immigration. Yet the solution is, in light of what we now know, not a question of more officials, more fences and more patrol boats. Rather, why do people want to move? Why do peopl e not respect others as a matter of course? What are the systemic causes of these problems? That is the fundamental agenda.

Much is made about authorities 'finding the will' to effect solutions, a will for which we wait a long, long time. The fundamental point is not a q uestion of will, for it is both elusive and illusory. The focus needs to shift to costs: specifically, the costs of resistance as opposed to the costs of adaptation and change. Peace is about adaptation. For authorities at all levels, peace is about order, manifested as control. 'Crime' demands that we have more prisons. In the contemporary language of business culture, 'our people are ou r most important asset' and the personnel department gave way to 'Human Resources' – an d employees over-managed and burdened with systems of accountability, bureaucratized and stressed, with all th e accumulated costs associated therewith, direct and otherwise.

In summary, systems of peaceful relations are, fundamentally and authentically, person-centric, whilst they are also simultaneously humano-centric, especially in t he context of a social cosmology that was radically revealed to us forty years ago: we are a s mall, vulnerable ball (an d a rath er dirty one at th at) spinning in space. The concept of peace relates to s elf-realization, emancipation (and, important though the literature of gender is, it is a transitory phenomenon, a means to emancipation) and the satisfaction of needs, not the contesting of rights.

Organizations are means, not ends, yet they appear to have become ends in themselves, states not excepted. We delude ourselves if we continue to adhere to the idea of the statist pretence: namely, that because we invented the state and have lived with it for a few centuries, then somehow we have reached the highest and most advanced form of human socio-political evolution. For many on the planet, where the state is not an impediment, it is an irrelevance.

Chapter 6

Issues of Significance

In this penultimate chapter, against a b ackground that investigates the origins of Peace Research, the means of projection via the journals and a s urvey of its substantive concerns, we survey a s et of issues that not on ly emanate the enterprise, but also draw in appropriate issues from similarly critical sources, effectively to giv e us the outline of a co ntinuing agenda of study. The cluster of nine features addressed here is not an exhaustive list and others may want to see a different cluster. Nevertheless, they try to summarize the major issues.

1.   On the Survival of Peace Research

This is the most obvious thing we can say about Peace Research. Despite all th e hazards and pitfalls along the way, not only has the enterprise survived, it has grown and flourished. At the outset and many times since, many have seen it as naïve, a mixture of hope and expectation, but truly flying in the face of political realities, not only related to the here and now, but also to the persistent and inescapable condition of being human, as rev ealed by the historical record. But Peace Research has been extraordinarily audacious, indeed courageous, in assaulting not only the weight of the established canon, but also its authority. That was an observation made at the outset of this work and it is worthy of repetition here.

Many, undoubtedly, saw the Peace Researchers as naïve, perhaps dismissing them in light of their personal beliefs, as pacifist or Q uaker or radi cal. From an alternative perspective, the very nature of the personal stance – so often constructed with difficulty and introspection – came to be so strong that it was one from which they would not be shifted. They were, many of them, convinced of the nature of the stance – and the nature of the problem to de addressed, whether it be militarism, the arbitrary nature of authority as exercised (political and/or intellectual) and the conditions associated with being human in the twentieth century. In that they sought to change things, then predictably many of them came to be self-selecting members of the 'awkward squad' or the usual suspects. Some saw them as subversive, an many of them were, for they sought to attack the foundations of the conventional wisdom. On occasion, they were deemed to be tendentious. The 1980s debate about Peace Studies twenty years ago in Britain stands as an example.

Often, relationships amongst scholars were informal and invisible. Funding was always a major problem and still is for many. There is n ow an evident visibility, but the geographical spread across the globe is uneven. There are firm foundations in, for example, Scandinavia, Germany and the United States where the record is impressive. In Britain, there are only a handful of institutional bases, as is the case in France. National 'style' and culture are important considerations. Institutional politics are also important. Indeed, even though the University of Bradford initiative received much attention at its foundation thirty years ago, there was still a degree of apprehension with regard to the financing of universities n general, and 'last in' first out' was a preferred strategy for some. In some places, it was a case of retreat, with the Peace Research Centre in Canberra, Australia a casualty. The same fate befell the Richardson Institute in London, though it has a presence at Lancaster University.

In a sense, there is a certain predictability about all of this that really should not surprise us. There are countless examples of instances where novelty has been resisted and dismissed. This, say the defenders looking at the emergent assaults on their academy, is not what the subject is about. What is proposed is said to be facile, marginal or irrelevant and, besides, we are doing it already, even though it may not seem so. For Peace Research, read Gender Studies, Cultural Studies and so on. The problem is that emergent novelties are not easily perceived from existing perceptual lenses. That being the case, the novelty is reduced to the form or aspect of that which we do know and can explain. The strategy of defence then becomes a mixture of reduction, to that which is known, and assertion, that this is the case. However, the persistence and growth of alternative approaches and perspectives are instrumental in demonstrating, not asserting, the essential aspects of the existing paradigm.

2.   PR as Rejectionist

Peace Research found its origins in the era of nuclear confrontation of the 1950s where some contemplated the use of nuclear weapons in defence of US interests. Insofar as that issue is now back on the agenda of political choice, despite the end of the Cold War (or because of it?) we have, bizarrely, come full circle. However, there has been a consistent theme, then and now, of a fundamental rejection of the nuclear weapon in particular, together with policies that envisage its threat and use.

It is remarkable that, in pursuit of stable deterrence, options for decision-makers (such as the range of choices presented under the guise of the policy of 'flexible response') and promises to allies, many thousands of weapons were deployed. The strategy of flexible response led to a process, as between the United States and the Soviet Union, of essential force matching, a de facto process of proliferation. It is no coincidence that the five permanent members of the UN Security Council are all declared nuclear-weapon states. Israel has not declared its status, but it known to have a considerable stock of nuclear weapons. India and Pakistan are in possession of such weapons. Moreover, it is interesting to note the somewhat questionable stance of the state(s) which possess weapons of mass destruction; there is an implicit assumption that weapons in their possession are held in responsible and secure hands. The spread of these weapons would, necessarily, see them come into the possession of those of moral dubiety and questionable responsibility. There is no logic to this stance, save an elitism that many resent.

Peace Researchers reject the nuclear paradigm in particular and the Strategic Studies paradigm in general. More s pecifically, there is a rej ection of the very notions that the weapons and threats can deter; t hat they rest on untested and essentially unknowable premises and that their utility is morally questionable, as are the outcomes that they produce. The questions of deterrence received much attention in the literature, especially in the early years of the Journal of Conflict Resolution. The psychology of deterrence was much studied, together with the role of armaments. The Weber-Fechner Law demonstrated that there was no linearity in the nature of threats; in other words, a threat had to be ten times as destructive to have twice the deterrent effect. Indeed, they might not even deter at all. Yet it was assumed that if an event had not happened, then this was due to deterrence. So, since the Soviet Union had not invaded Western Europe, this was because they had been deterred by the existence of weapons in Europe.

Insofar as Peace Research has expanded beyond the agenda of nuclear weapons, it has encompassed other socio-political practices, consistent with the address of conflict as a generic phenomenon, without special claims to uniqueness in one realm as opposed to another. Take the case of punishment and imprisonment in society. With specific respect to th e United States, Angela Davis has made a series of observations that are truly astonishing, not only in the sheer fact of their revelation, but the practices that are rev ealed. In the late 1960s the prison population in the United States was of the order of 200,000; it is now of the order of two million. Indeed, with one-twentieth of the world's population, the United States is responsible for two-ninths of the world's total prison population. Between 1984 and 1989, nine new prisons were constructed in the state of California alone. The mood, from the Reagan presidency onwards, was that communities were to be rendered safe, sine authorities would be 'tough on crime.' However 'the practice of mass incarceration during that period had little o r no effect on official crime rates…larger prison populations led to larger prison populations' (Davis 2003 pp.11-13). The former Chief Inspector of Prisons in Britain, David Ramsbotham, wrote about the state of British prisons in 2003, g iving his book' Prisongate' the rather more revealing subtitle 'the shocking state of Britain's Prisons and the need for visionary change' (Ramsbotham 2003). In her review of the book, Marian FitzGerald observed that his conclusions 'are by no means original: many feature in report after report going back more than twenty years; but most have foundered on a system which defaults to a strategy of inertia/ (FitzGerald 2003 p.8).

Of course these are observations are not strictly Peace Research, as it were; they do not come out or P eace Research Institutes or j ournals. Nevertheless, they add synergies to the Peace Research agenda, inform it a nd add weight to the case that is being made. In being rejectionist, Peace Researchers are not alone in being so. The problems, across the boundaries of academic divisions, mount up. More to the point, the problems are not bein g solved because they are in capable of being solved using conventional assumptions, institutions and practices. This is c lear from the evidence with regard to current system performance, of which these are but two, but it is also clear th at, in being rejectionist, Peace Research has researched for alternatives. Behaviour can be changed without strategies and policies of threat and coercion. Moreover, where threat and punishment are resorted to, they frequently have deleterious effects: either making the problem addressed worse rather than better; or creat ing new problems that are pass ed on for some other authority or agency to address. Recidivism amongst offenders is a case in point.

The point here is t hat traditional policies are q uestionable in their foundations and in their consequences. In pursuit of control, we threaten. If the threat is not heeded, we threaten more with more weapons, and so on, on the presumption that this will work and bring about security.

3.   Peace Research as Innovation

So, Peace Research has survived and it has rejected much that passed for knowledge associated with peace, war and conflict. And then what? Insofar as Peace Research had, and has, at it s centre the dimensions of human conflict conceived as problems, then the task has been to seek solutions through re-search, using appropriate methods and an eclectic stance.

The standard challenge to the critic has been to come up with an alternative. The Peace Research community has devoted a great deal of effort to doing so. The accumulated record of respectable, rigorous, detailed an d cumulative research is there ready for inspection. It is certainly too serious and rigorous to be dismissed as 'alternative' these days.

Thus, we now know that it is not a ca se of simple separation into domestic and international politics, with associated notions of uniqueness and non-comparability. If our focus is on human behaviour, with the clear comcomitant that what is important is a pers pectives on the systems of communication and interaction that transcend formal system boundaries, then we see the phenomenon of human behaviour as generic in form and pattern. There are h omologies; what applies in one realm can be applied in others. This has been a key achievement of the last forty years or s o of inn ovative thought associated with what it is that people actually do in relation to each other.

To repeat, there has been an inherent task-expansion; peace has not been the absence of some things; it is necessarily the presence of others. In other words, the behavioural foundations of peace need to be re- constituted consistent with new findings. Clearly these findings are vast, from the cultural foundations of societies where conflict is rife to t hose which can properly be des cribed as peaceful (see Melko 1972). At the other end of the spectrum, we now have technical manuals that demonstrate, in quite specific terms, the rules of conflict resolution strategies and procedure, for third-parties and facilitators. There has, thus, been a process of discovery, refinement and fabrication. What Burton, Banks, Mitchell and Groom (and others) were doing in London from about 1969 in terms of, first conflict and communication, and then further refined versions of that initial approach has become a new approach that is o f practical utility. As Mitchell and Banks have observed 'this handbook is intended to be pract ical, brief and forthright, buts origins are exactly the opposite. It is the result of thirty years of academic research, originally of an abstract and theoretical kind but increasingly, during the 1980s and 1990s involving practical interventions into protracted and deep-rooted conflicts, partly with the objective of testing out the usefulness of that theoretical work' (Mitchell and Banks 1996 p.vii). In other words there has been some experience of actual conflict transformation and a distillation of the methods and procedures and transformations.

Which is to make the point in two ways. We do not need to re-invent the wheel when, in conventional terms, a 'new' problem turns up. Second, though the achievements of Peace Research do n ot yet include the achievement of a s table world peace, there are many and significant cases of successful conflict resolution, as opposed to unsuccessful attempts at repression and control.

4. Peace Education as Instrument and Goal

The appearance of works such as the Mitchell and Banks manual is testimony to the stage of evolution that is represented by the explicit attention paid to peace education. This takes many forms.

The first thing to say is that it is now possible for students to graduate with degrees in Peace Studies, Peace and Justice Studies and the like. This is itself a remarkable achievement. A nod in the direction of relevance will not do: university procedures demand that explicit attention be paid to co re concerns, aims and objectives, learning development and progression, assessment and associated questions. For both staff and students, a rigorous attention to discipline is over-riding consideration. Validation procedures demand rigorous attention, not only to detail but to con tent and structure. That there are u ndergraduate degrees is symptomatic of one stage of development and maturity, a process taken two steps further with the appearance of postgraduate degrees and, especially, Ph.D. degrees. The latter presumes the existence of those who are competent to supervise, as well as those who are competent to examine to the required standard. These are being done and universities and colleges are increasingly awarding qualifications to thise who reach the appropriate s tandard. This is in itself notable; Ph.D. in Peace Research/Peace Studies is a major achievement from a subject thought to be 'respectable' as recently as 1969.

So what do these people do? Do they go out into the world and 'do peace?' Not, quite, in the sense that one might go out into the world of industry and commerce and practise physics or chemistry. Nor can every competent graduate find a teach ing position were they wont to do so. Yet more and more do, as institutions enhance what Peace Research has to of fer and include that in the curriculum, surely a sign of relevance and change. So what do these people do, who are newly qualified? There is no typical or straightforward set of answers, but some would include counseling, police service, mediation services, community roles in organizations that have proliferated, not to mention involvement with the massively-increased numbers of non-state actors that are part of the domain of global politics at the start of the twenty-first century. And agents of social change and response have evolved as u ntreated socio-political problems have gone unsolved and, in due course, demanded attention. The point to make is that frequently there is no obvious point of impact and there is no obvious immediate or signal set of 'effects.' Change is most significant where it is g radual, incremental and fundamental: which usually takes time. Changes in procedures are o ften deemed disruptive and resisted. Changes in cultures are often clear in retrospect, so that participants are not exactly aware of when they stopped doing one thing and started doing another.

Clearly there is a corpu s of work that straddles the boundary between education and training. That which is learned can als o be applied in specific circumstances. There are t echniques and there is a framework of general applicability that can be brought to bear across a range of socio-political situations. Apart from that which can be taught, there is also much that can be learned, in terms of rules as well as skills. There is clear evidence, and 'case law' nowadays, of the successes of alternative dispute resolution down to family level and neighbour disputes. These are not, yet, the commonest practices, but nor are they rare. At the other end of the spectrum, a topic t hat has received (and continues to receive) attention is the idea of an 'alternative' international civil service, trained in the principles and practices of conflict analysis and resolution. These might constitute a facility-in-being, ready and able to act at a g iven stage of an emergent conflict (perhaps when a set of early-warning indicators showed that a conflict was entering a decis ive stage), to in tervene to decis ive effect. This is an interesting innovation, certainly radical in terms its potential, not to mention the threat that this represents to not only established practices, but also with respect to principles of intervention in international behaviour.

The question of peace ed ucation is not a new one and it has long been controversial. Education for, say, geography or geology seems sound and acceptable. Even, with regard to the social sciences, economics and sociology are taught in schools. Where questions relating to war and peace are add ressed, they have tended to be addres sed via the perspective of history principally, not least since it is the perspective with which children in schools are most familiar and comfortable. Shephard et al (1993) stands a good example from a British source. The book carries the title 'Peace and War' and appeared in the context of the Schools History Project, established in 1972 by the Schools Council. It addresses key relevant questions: how did the holocaust happen? Was the dropping of the atomic bomb justified? It is serious material appropriately dealt with.

So we must ask the question why, a decade earlier, th ere was such a furore when it was suggested that peace studies might be in troduced into the school curriculum. The issue received unusual publicity, even making the television news and a front page or two. The matter was thought to be too controversial, especially in the context of the-then current crisis associated with the NATO cruise missile controversy. Understandable, of course. But it did touch a nerve.

Undoubtedly, much of this has to do with what Perry Anderson once labeled 'the components of national culture' (Anderson 1992) with respect specifically to the British case. Yet t he notion has more general applicability. Especially in relation to education, there are significant questions of a national and a c ultural nature. In the Spring of 2005, t ensions increased between China and Japan, ostensibly about the writing of school history books in Japan which omitted mention of Japanese behaviour during the 1930s invasion of China. As to national preferences and styles more generally, presumably the French would wish that more attention be paid to Marianne and Napoleon, rather than Betsy Ross and George Washington.

Yet, in 2005, in 'the global village' and a world getting smaller owing to the processes of globalization/mondialisation, we need to ask the question 'education for what?' In part, this has been answered, to the effect that we need to educate our children so as to equip the with the skills necessary for 'us' to compete and 'hold our own' in an increasingly competitive world, where emergent economies represent serious 'challenges.' In Britain this has given rise to the National Curriculum, with associated targets set for acquired competence at 'key stages' in terms of reading, mathematics and the like. Fine, as far as it goes. But this has had knock-on effects, with other areas squeezed out, some would argue. And where is the scope for innovation? Yes, there is provision for the learning of 'life and social skills' and 'citizenship' but it is, likewise, a matter of some dispute as to whether or not there is adequate provision devoted to sex education in a time of social concern.

In summary, much has been done, but much more still remains to be done, in difficult circumstances. Nevertheless, having already raised the question as to the imperatives to change and the costs of resistance, we might raise another tension: the extant journals of peace education are addressing the nature of the necessary and desirable. How long can they be held to be marginalized or peripheral to the emergent realities and problems of national stance and a global agenda?

5.   The Question of Culture

The concerns of Peace Research necessarily involve a consideration of the cultures of war and the cultures (actual or potential) of peace, not least because it is part of the task of culture to reproduce itself as part of the life-stance, of group, community, nation or state. At the same time, we need to recognize the wider implications of the question of culture.

In the operation of a states-system, nationalism has permitted, fostered and legitimized the development of difference, as an inherent feature of the system. With the growth of globalization, a central question being addressed is whether and to what extent this phenomenon of globalization is a promise or threat of cultural change and whether or not this will lead to stances of cultural resistance. An allied concern is the extent to which globalization is but one manifestation of Capitalism in general or American capitalism in particular.

The demands of nationalism and national identity dictate that history gets to be written in a particular war, which is to say selectively (because not everything can be written in). Indeed, there is the somewhat controversial question as to whether we can speak of the world having 'a history' separate from the histories of its component parts, conceived as states and other entities. That aside, we recognize that the construction of history prioritizes, categorizes and, in consequence, gives rise to a set of values, embodied as choices and stored as 'social' or 'national' or et hnic values. And these are deem ed to matter, because they are 'felt.' At its crudest, the question of culture, identity and difference is a simple one: them and us. And where there is no collected memory as embodied in tradition, then it ca n be created or imagined (for two very different, but complementary, treatments, see Hobsbawm and Ranger 1983 and Hynes 1992). All of his is part of the creation, reproduction and memory associated with identity.

Is it all under threat in light of the apparent inexorable force of globalization, where there are global icons, labels, symbols and the associated identity symbols in the era of late-capitalism and post-modernity? Is culture an impediment or a treasure?

We know that 'culture' is an elusive concept, but we know aspects of it when we see it. Beethoven and Goya are thought to be 'culture' just as Rap and Tracy Emin or Damian Hirst are thought not to be by the overwhelming majority. What, in a post-modern world, constitutes culture is a major debate which proceeds.

What is easier to grasp are the central elements of what we might call the war-peace agenda. In cannot be gainsaid that what is reproduced is consequential for our constructions of 'self 'and 'otherness.' The latter is more easily addressed than the former. For the British post-1945 generation of c hildren, otherness was what was reproduced in comics and on the cinema screen. Comics depicted ou r chaps as heroes and Germans as villains, wnd with a restricted vocabulary to boot. It seemed that the vocabulary of the average German – who just happened to be a soldier – ran to Englander, Himmel! and Achtung! and little beyond that. The stereotypical German was precisely that: even as recently as 'The Great Escape', directed by John Sturges and based on Paul Brickhill's book, when the camp commander appeared to be   too len ient, and not quite as per s tereotype, a stereotypical commander appeared. And why should this be important? Because it seems to get an annual showing on British television, as traditional family viewing.

To nobody's great surprise, the Second World War s pawned hundreds of films devoted to its d epiction, re-enactment and the like. Vietnam was to do likewise. But with what consequences? As recently as April 2005, th e German ambassador in London told the BBC that he feared that a failure of the British to engage with modern and more relevant images of Germany might lead to a deterioration in the relationship in the longer term. We can see what he meant, especially when he recounted that most British schoolchildren could name only one German; and it was not Beethoven.

Culture is not only about that which is th ought to be of value and which should persist. It also creates expectations – and it simplifies. At the height of the East-West tensions in the 1980s, a pos ter was popular, made in the style of the classic Hollywood western; the Good Guy (in the white hat) got the Girl and the Bad Guy (in the Black Hat) got what was comin' to him! Reagan and Thatcher on the one hand, Brezhnev on the other. In the cinema which it parodied, that was always the outcome. Even John Wayne was moved to make his own 'Vietnam movie' (The Green Berets) which had an ending unlike any other of the treatments of the war: the Asian boy, with an American arm around his shoulder walked into the sunset.

Now all o f this is co nsequential for the way it str uctures, interprets and creates the picture, as it were. Sometimes these cultural products give rise to widely-shared assumption that there is a solution: years after John Wayne, along came Tom Cruise in 'Top Gun;' not only did he defeat the (faceless, because covered in a black mask) enemy, he made friends with the man he did not like, lost his best buddy along the way – and got the girl at the end of the film. Yet there have been very few images of casualties coming out of Iraq since 2003, as there were from Vietnam. Which is to say that the point makes itself. Images of war are controversial, sensitive to some and, undoubtedly, politically sensitive. If the British conflict in the Falklands in 1982 gave us the selected correspondents (only two went with the British Task Force), the 2003 intervention Iraq gave us the 'embedded correspondent' and it is tempting to suggest that the information content of the reports was in inverse proportion to its duration.

If images produced in westerns and war films reproduced stereotype of what the man had to do and the wife who had to suffer as she must, then they were entirely products of their times and places. Roles and structures were clearly depicted and unambiguous at that. Until the spaces for a wider debate opened up in the 1960s, conformity was very much the order of the day. In Britain, when changes did come about, they gave rise to novel cultural forms, such as the 'kitchen-sink drama' as opposed to the comings and goings in the drawing room; the 'angry young men' now demanded to be heard. As did the Beat Generation in the United States. Once the spaces for debate were opened up, they were soon full and wider in consequence. Conformity was no longer the order of the day, where girls played with dolls and boys with guns.

The new cultural spaces became cultural challenges to the dominant ethos, with regard to then little understood questions of gender, subculture and the like. These have been referred to in passing in much of the foregoing and stand in no need of repetition here. So what did it all amount to? The challenges prompted not only self-examination, but precipitated new approaches to social analysis, later embodied in Cultural Studies (see McRobbie 2005 for a recent interpretation), Gender Studies and Feminism. Like Peace Research, they interrogated the conventional discourse, with the intention to subvert the power of conventional norms and effect changes, not only the discourse but also in the politics that the discourse both represented on the one hand and challenged on the other.

Significantly, the discipline of International Relations, coping as it must with the implications of globalization has also reached out – at least a part of it – to with the question of culture through an engagement with the idea of not only the Military Industrial Complex, but also the Media, Military Industrial Complex. The agenda is significant with regard to the question of creation, reproduction and political significance of the various media.

6. The Quality of Life

The quality that has made 'modern man' modern is our control of the environment. We have harnessed such power as we have been able to develop with a view to improving the material conditions of life on the planet, at least for some of the people some of the time. Masterless man was modern man. Material advancement was our goal and economic growth was our yardstick of success; distribution of wealth was a secondary question, for nothing could be (re)distributed without its prior creation. So th ere was a g oal so self-evident that it was not at all controversial: growth was a clear and present task, a promise.

However, and certainly with regard to the experiences of the advanced states which have, by and large accumulated wealth, this has created more problems, that are difficult to get to grips with. Though much has been written about Third World debt, there is now the problem of accumulated consumer debt in mature economies. This has given rise to anxieties in finance ministries, outweighed only by the weight and breadth of anxiety amongst their publics. We have accumulated more and more, despite or perhaps in light of changing financial orthodoxies, yet there has been an evident lack of well-being, indeed more anxiety, stress and manifest insecurity.

We have the means travel the g lobe, yet fear terrorist attack. We have (at least many of us) have opted for the huge 4x4 and justified the choice by asserting that is makes us feel secure. We waste our time on roads that are full, fearful of a frustrated, who might attack us out of a fit of 'road rage.' We eng age others indirectly, through the media. We vacate the traditional spaces of encounter in cities and towns, for they are the spaces of risk, real or imagined.

Something is wrong here. More has given rise to the very perverse view that more is less. We lament the loss of community. 'In the face of the fabulous promises of economic growth, at the start of the 21st century we are confronted by an awful fact. Despite high and sustained levels of economic growth in the West over a period of 50 y ears – g rowth that has seen average real in comes increase several times over – the mass of people are no more satisfied with their lives now than they were then. If growth is intended to give us better lives, and there can be no other purpose, it has failed' (Hamilton 2003 p.3).

This notion of 'quality of life' was addressed in the journal 'New Scientist' in October 2003. There Bond reiterated Hamilton's point o the effect that 'one of the most significant observations is that in industrialized nations, average happiness has remained virtually static since the Second World War, despite a considerable rise in average income. The exception is Denmark...no one is quite sure why'(Bond 2003 p.42). Moreover, 'there is another twist. The happiest nations – m ostly western and individualistic ones – al so tend to have the highest levels of suicide.' Quoting from a rece nt work by Kasser (2002), Bond took the case even further, since Kasser found that 'young adults who focus on money, image and fame tend to be more depressed, have less enthusiasm for life and suffer more physical symptoms such as sore throats and headaches than others. A further source to add weight to the case was Richard Layard from the Centre for Economic Performance at the London School of Economics, who argued that the pursuit of social status at the level of society was 'totally fruitless.' Since it gave rise such things as league tables – with many failing as well as those who do succeed, then 'this condemns as many to fail as to succeed; not a good formula for raising personal happiness.'

And all of this, in the context of ostensible functioning and 'peaceful' societies, bt where there are concerns about the proliferation of sub-cultures, some of them violent, others less violent but still antisocial. In Britain, the response of the authorities was to institute the device of the Anti-Social Behaviour Order (ASBO), to prevent and restrain certain sorts of behaviour. Yes, quite so, but surely a question, again, of symptoms and causes.

Something is seriously at fault: our assumptions about what constitute appropriate indicators. It is surely no exaggeration to say that though systems are not failing at everything, since we are not in a descent into anarchy yet, too many systems are failing at too many things, globally and locally. War, violent conflict, exploitation, alienation, anomie, degradation (of self, community and the environment), commodification, and the rest are cumulative in their effects. The responses of the wealthiest amongst us? The proliferation of secure and gated communities.

There are, still, collective goods that we value, but the production of collective 'bads' is inceasingly the point.

7. Towards a Culture of Peace

All of the foregoing is by way of a prelude to the question, 'what of the nature of not only a process of peace, but what is the nature of a culture of peace'? Many will assert that this is illusory and Utopian for, it is asserted, there will always be bullies who respect only overwhelming force, which will, perforce, be required, now and always. But bullies and dictators are created by circumstances, psychological predispositions notwithstanding. We know the constituent parts of what is required in the project: a sense of self, need satisfaction, participation, authenticity, legitimacy, community, relationships, sustainability, respect for difference.

It might, therefore, be useful to explore the extent to which individuals, groups and societies are predisposed to act associatively; in other words, to reverse the usual supposition that people are associative in light of likely penalties if they were not. We behave as we do since we fear retribution, arrest and threats of punishment. Yet many people associate with others because they have similar needs, values and responsibilities. They also cooperate to the greater individual and social good, feeling that this is the essential attribute of being a 'social being' as well as a human being. To repeat, again, we may have made the most profound error in assuming that children learn through measures of control; that criminals respond to a cost-benefit analysis of likely arrest and detention, calculating resultant profit and loss; that states are deterred by threats of punishment and so on. How can we know when threat and coercion work and, more fundamentally, whether they are relevant strategies of control and conformity?

Usually, it is asserted that this is so, because it is so, obviously. Nothing is obvious and much is contestable, not least the validity of practices based in history that were once deemed right and proper. But times change and so, too, do relevant contexts. Thus, we would be well advised to assume that the future will not be like the past, but will need careful assessment and preparation, rather than incremental tumbling into some future period.

How, then, can we prepare for a culture of peace? First, we can assume that is possible. Second, that is likely. Third, that it may be infinitely more useful and functional that the one we have. Fourth, that it will be a s ocial order th at is legitimate in its relationships and consensual in its p rocedures. Needs, rights and responsibilities will be articulated and recognized. And it might, just, be less-costly than the system we currently have.

And what will be instrumental in bringing all o f this about? First, th e recognition that a zero-sum approach to socio-political problems is a nachronistic, at a ti me when the interconnectedness of t he globe is clear for all to s ee, in its expressions of violence, trade, com munication, migration and so on. This means that competitive and decisive policies of 'me first' need to be assessed in terms of the damage that they cause, in the immediate, medium and long term. To take but one issue; it has been said that the United Sta tes is a s pecial place a nd that its prosperity is not negotiable. Specialness may be a s hort term preoccupation; long-term prosperity will have to be becau se it is related to a systemic dynamic of dominance and dependence that many more around the world are contesting, one way or the other.

Security is a col lective good. In an era of globalization, the idea of 'homeland security' is a cont radiction in terms. In an era of globalization, there may be an advancing ethic of global responsibility, consequent upon an added dimension of transparency. The military means to security are q uestionable, in terms of their cost, efficacy, consequences and limitations. The Iraq in vasion of 2003 is a case in point; 'mission accomplished' was proclaimed in May 2003 and casualties continued to mount through the remainder of the year, so that the key issue, for the United States especially, was more concerned with an exit strategy rather than anything else. There is e vidently still no end to the question of optimistic intelligence estimates and expectations of short wars. Many assumed that 'shock and awe' allied to 'shoot and scoot' would see a war over in days. They were to be disappointed, but determined, presumably, to do better next time.

A culture of peace is not based on the absence of conflict. Conflict is not valued for itself, nor is it to be inculcated into individuals (children as well as adults) as a short and simple way to get what we want. We can learn cooperation, sharing and ways of resolving conflict effectively, without malice, revenge and the like. And we now know that conflict is functional in certain circumstances.

This not 'pie in the sky.' There is e vidence that we can inhabit a world of possibilities, not one of inevitabilities. We have the means, the instruments and, most fundamental of all, we have the knowledge that can inform the possibilities.

8.   The Question of Time, Change and Future

If, as we have argued, authorities, structures and systems of power have resorted to means of coercion as strategies of control, then a corollary of that is that short-term considerations related to control and resistance to change figure high on the agenda of policy choices. Order is the prim ary goal and questions of change, future and long-term consequences are releg ated to th e status of s econdary or tertiar y importance. This stance will increasingly prove to be unsustainable and counter-productive. The future is not simply an incremental accumulation of todays and tomorrows. The future also has a dynamic and a consequence.

We need to address the extent to which the future represents an opportunity for unlimited 'progress'. Moreover, we need to qu estion what 'progress' means. The faith in scientific progress and technological development may lead some to the view that where solutions are n ot within our grasp, then they soon will be. After all, it was suggested that London would be f eet deep i n horse manure by 19xx, but this did n ot eventuate because we were able to m ake progress. That approach may be limited in time and space: we may not find space on the moon or Mars and we may be moving incrementally towards a f uture which threatens Dystopia rather than any more benign alternative.

In the future, where do we think, as a human race, we want to be? (see, for example, Cooper and Layard 2001) Are we convinced that we have a future on this planet, or do we hope and expect that we will have a future because we have a past and a present? Of course, we have evolved and we feel that we have a momentum allied to the hope of a boun dless and bountiful future. Technology is only one of the relevant dimensions. We h ave found mastery of science and the development of technological means much easier than we have progress in the realm of human relationships. We have sought security through wars and found it elusive. We have sought peace th rough strength and nuclear deterrence and found it illus ory. We have sought to control our neighbours by threats and fences, laws and edicts and found them unwilling to bend to our desires. Others have been persistent in the expression of their sense of self and otherness, much to our discomfiture. Where they transgress, we punish. Where they threaten, we deter. But technological solutions will not solve the underlying problems. 'It is too soon to tell whether that [electronic] "age" will even survive the next century...Of far greater importance to our survival will be avoiding the social trap of supposing that pseudo-communities – whether gangs on the street, encounter groups or "virtual communities" on the internet – are adequate substitutes for real people in real places sharing meaningful lives. In whatever forms the commoditization of human caring comes, be it through centralized welfare systems or payment for personal services, it tends to be destructive of real community and hence of real human beings' (Clark 2003 p.404).

If we approach the future as we have conducted ourselves in the past, then our survival on the planet is not assured. There are limits to what is possible in the absence of change. The proliferation of surplus capacities in competitive industries is wasteful, irrational and damaging to the world's environment. The harvesting of, say, timber as a short-cut to income generation or the preservation of sectoral employment is short-sighted and may be di sastrous in the short-term. Massive mudslides in Asia and Latin America are often attributed to deforestation on upper slopes of mountain ranges, which permits and encourages rapid run-off, floods and the like. We have treated the motor car as a m eans of liberation and so it is, in the micro. We can reconstruct our day and night, entertain or insulate ourselves on the way to work and avoid certain hazards. But all of this is consequential in the macro, giving rise to pollution, resource depletion and a rel iance on short-term solutions, such as road widening. These will not deal with the underlying problems.

In this sense, the political implications of the new planetary ontology have yet to be translated into a serious political agenda to deal with accumulated long-term consequences. Bear in mind that the Industrial Revolution took place less than three hundred years ago in Europe. The large-scale and widespread consumerization of India and China has yet to take place, with consequences that can only, now, be guessed at. States and governments are still locked into the essential principles of the Westphalian system of states; they acknowledge no authority higher than themselves, they are bound by their own interests and their own sense of security – which is at risk.

Except that security is now indivisible. The Brandt Commission was instrumental in raising the profile of common security in global discourse and it was notable that Mikhail Gorbachev was moved to try to recast the agenda of European security in terms of a 'common European home.' Against the background of modern European history, and the lessons of more modern European integration, this was a significant initiative in itself. There has been no similar breakthrough at the global level to this point. The Kyoto Protocol stands as a test and a testimony to failure; United States reservations mean that the process is at a dead end, in effect if not in the letter of the protocol.

This mind set cannot endure. Somewhere and at some time there will have to be a confrontation with the costs of resistance to change and the benefits of adaptation. The stance of essential stasis will be unstable and, in all likelihood, promote conflict, and perhaps violent conflict. Claims of specialness, exceptionalism and prior interests will not be sufficient. Indeed, there might come a time not only when we recognize that posterity matters, but that an obligation to the poor, needy and desperate is a cost worth paying by the rich (in light of the possible alternatives) for living collectively. Currently, many of the costs associated with the activities of the developed West are not properly addressed, never mind met. Aircraft fuel, the very life-blood of travel and tourism, carries no tax. We need a radical re-assessment of our cost-of-living, but in a planetary sense. Otherwise, the wealthy may choose to live a life of isolation, in (notional) conditions of security, but psychologically distressed and prepared for violence.

We would be well advised to turn in on ourselves, certainly the fortunate amongst us, to address a very simple but hugely important question – or two; what do we think that the future is for? And, consequent upon that, how do we think that we shall get there? Leave it to the children – or construct a new politics of obligation as an existential priority, no more and no less. One thing is certain, the future cannot resemble the past. There is a literature to assist us in the task of getting from here to there (Adam 1995, Elise Boulding 1988, Boulding and Boulding 1995). First of all there is the recognition of responsibility and the role of custodianship of the future. Secondly, there is a literature of creative futures, some of it associated with the World Order Models Project and which is rooted in a series of multicultural perspectives. Thirdly, there is the agenda of economic resource managenment, where it is clear that resources are finite, at least many of them that matter. Fourthly, there is the literature associated with not only the costs of economic growth but als o the social limitations to economic growth. Advertising and the selling of 'aspirational lifestyle goals' can only be for the few, by definition, even though they are 'sold' to the many. Yet some people will live under the flight paths of aircraft at busy airports, some will live near motorways or be prone to pollution. We are, thus, now paying a high price for 'commodities' that were once free for all, at no cost: such as peace and quiet, clean air, a sight of trees or the sea. In many places, beaches are private with limited or public access. In coastal areas New South Wales, south of Sydney in Australia, beach homes with a view of the sea are selling for more than one million dollars, and they are often an far from palatial.

Thus, we have to ask, how far can this process of commodification go in an interdependent globe, with finite space (and even where low-lying Pacific islands are threatened with submersion under rising sea levels), limited resources and growing populations? As with questions of prisons and nuclear weapons, just how much is enough, when 'more' is no answer?

Chapter 7

Observations in Place of a Conclusion

It would be inappropriate to head these remarks with the heading 'Conclusion' for we are assessing a work in progress. The stress in the title of the work is on the first fifty years. It may be that it will run on to another anniversary in another fifty years, under the same rubric. What is certain is that if Peace Research disappeared as a separate entity it would not disappear without trace. There is too much accumulated evidence, empirical and otherwise, as well as a conceptual map and an alternative lexicon of relationships, structures and processes that are now central to how we think about conflict, war and peace.

Yet we might also entertain the notion that if, as we have argued, Peace Research is rejectionist, innovative and instrumental, then its disappearance as a discrete and identifiable entity could be seen as a mark of its own success. That work subsumed under the rubric 'that awful phrase' would then be part of a wider, holistic approach to the study of human behavior at all levels of social relationships and interaction, from the small interpersonal (intra- inter-familial, for example) to more complex, but essentially similar, and thus comparable, relations at the global level. We have, at least, established that conflict is a generic phenomenon. In other words, Peace Research would have been instrumental in effecting a shift of paradigm, away from International Politics and towards something entirely more relevant and all-encompassing. It might share this task of effecting paradigm shift with other recent innovations in scholarship, say Cultural Studies and Feminist/Women's Studies. Both of these were ridiculed as 'non'subects' at first appearance, probably symptoms of intellectual trendyness and/or political correctness. Yet, over time, both have deomonstrated the limitations of the conventional wisdom. A study of any social phenomenon without a consideration of gender would be partial at best and probably misleading. Women have a role, a past, a history and a key place in life and in discourse. Similarly, the question of culture is important, whether it is sustaining a cultural perspective which establishes a view of otherness and difference (which, by many, is held to be self-evidently 'true'), validates the role of war or seeks to establish a culture of peace. Culture has, for all its eclecticism, long been absent from the discourse of International Relations, though there have been significant innovations in recent years (for an interim assessment, see Dunn 1995).

There is still much to do and the 'accumulated wisdom' of 5,000 years and more is hardly quiescent; far from it. It is articulated with enthusiasm at the highest levels of authority. Consider the two following examples. Why, asks Thomas Powers, can great powers not get along? 'The answer...is that in international competition for power, where differences sometimes lead to war, what intelligence organizations do – all that huggermugger of the great game – may look like strife, buts it's the closest serious international rivals ever get to peace' (Powers 2001 p.54). And, secondly, a commentary on the nature of foreign policy after three years of the Administration of George W. Bush; 'They held that the world was a bad, dangerous place; that the nation-state was its most important constituent part; that power, especially military power, was the coin of the realm in such a world; that international organizations treaties only constrained the use of American power; and that, uniquely among nations, America's interest and ideals were one' (*The Economist* 2003 p.120).

In July 1996, John Burton addressed six-hundred assembled individuals at the IPRA Conference in Brisbane, Australia. Early on in his keynote address, he said, of the Peace Research community 'we are no longer a small and unwelcome minority in academe [but] we have in forty years made little impact on political thinking [and] there still remains tremendous confusion in the public mind (Burton 1996. p.3). It is hard to sustain the view that we have made a dramatic breakthrough in the time since Burton spoke.

It may be that one of the greatest failings of the Peace Research community is that it has failed to engage, inform and stimulate the wider community. This is an issue of some significance and one to which we shall return shortly. But is important to recognize that there is still massive resistance. At the official level, of state authorities and similar power elites in almost all organizations, there is a predictable and understandable resistance to novel thinking that threatens not only role-holders, but also the very roles in structures themselves. There is also a resistance amongst the wider public, many of whom feel fear in face of change and probably opt for a populist expression of belief in tried and trusted methods which, though they do not seem to be working, are thought not to work because they are not being implemented hard enough. Thus, there are cries for more discipline, more prisons, sometimes conscription into the armed forces ('to teach them discipline and respect') and the like. Yet there is a widespread fear, of what it is not precisely clear, in many developed societies, never mind underdeveloped societies.

Consider the following. In South Africa, armed compounds for the elderly and/or wealthy are now being built and advertised on radio and television. They represent havens in a troubled world (Rogers 2001). In the past decades we have seen the flight to the (wider and more far-flung, remote and thus secure) suburbs on the part of the aspiring and achieving middle-classes. The cities are left to the urban poor, where poverty is rife, isolation self-evidence, violence the norm and killing a means to settle inter-gang disputes or as a rite of passage to secure membership. There is a widely-shared lament that once 'respectable working-class districts' are now places where violent crime is the norm, usually among the racially-separated urban and rootless poor, where drugs are a means to escape or wealth or both. Consequently, there are 'no-go areas' not only in Johannesburg or Washington, D.C., but also in Manchester, Melbourne and Minneapolis.

As if this were not enough, many are frightened to go out of their own homes, even in their own streets and suburbs, after dark. In many suburbs and towns, the installation of lighting and alarms is a recent, and rapidly-growing, industry. High street shops now employ security guards and entrances and exits are fitted with alarms. Never mind airports and high visibility public buildings. We are talking about people in the spaces they normally inhabit as they go about their work – a nd play. Young women on university campuses in North America and beyond are routinely escorted hole after an evening's relaxation. To go home alone is, manifestly, too risky. Drinks are consumed from bottles routinely: to drink from an unguarded glass is to run the risk of someone putting a drug into it and...?

In large cities and on buses and trains, it is routine to make oneself smaller, by tightening the body posture, read a book or newspaper, avoid physical contact and avoid eye contact. These are, whether we like it or n ot, the prevalent norms among many sections of, to reiterate, advanced wealthy and developed western societies. Many now prefer to travel by car, usually on their own, to feel that not only is it more convenient than (poorly provided) public transport, but that it is also safer, for we will then not have to encounter anyone we do not know, any or all of whom might, just might, be a t hreat. Children are, rou tinely, delivered to, a nd collected from, school by car, since parents are frightened that their children might to accosted or attacked by strangers. Never mind that more than 98% of children are harmed by people they know, usually family members or close friends. Parents know what they know and act on that knowledge: their children are safer in the car and, later, in th e home, rather th an playing in the street or recreation ground. Except that, as we now know, children 'safe' in the home are vulnerable to internet predators. And those who are driven to and from school are evidently prone to lack certain socializing skills and may be prone to weight problems because they lack sufficient exercise. This became a political issue in Britain in 2005.

Of crime and criminals, in all of this, it is clear the response is prison and punishment. For many, the longer the better, and the more severe the punishment the better. Yet we are entitled to ask whether this all works. Amongst young men in Britain, it is the case that the vat majority will re-offend within a short time of their release and be back in custody within two years. Many therefore infer that the problem is not in the principle of punishment buts its severity. If they re-offend, then they are n ot being punished enough in the first place, s o that it is quite obvious that punishment need to be even more severe. It is not that the policy fails; rather it is t hat it is not being implemented hard enough and with enough vigour, enthusiasms and determination. Thus, more prisons are built and more prisons are built...And so on. With the consequence, in the spirit of Foucault, people are reduced to the status of object, to be disciplined and punished.

So where do we go from here? The solution may be a conjunction of two trends, or discoveries.

First, authorities, in light of the consequences of policies being followed, will need to confront to issues: the accumulated costs of following current policies and, secondly, likely long-term consequences of following the existing policies. Consider the case of the conflict concerning Israel and Palestine. We have seen armed conflicts in 1948, 1956, 1967 and 1973; we are now three years and more into a s econd Intifada. Individuals are tar geted by missile-carrying helicopters, houses are b ulldozed and the casualties amongst civilians mount. On the Israeli side, individuals going about their ordinary business, in cafes and on buses are liable to be killed by suicide bombers, now both female and male. We can only wonder as to the quantity of tranquilizers and anti-depressant pills that are being consumed by the ordinary people in these circumstances. What is clear is that the various attempts and accords have been unsuccessful. 'Strong-men' leaders have been elected (f requently former soldiers, schooled in the ways of threat and coercion), determined to pu rsue coercive measures to bring about 'peace' which remains as elusive as ever. Walls are n ow in place to prevent contact between Palestinians and Israelis: these have also been tried in Belfast – as well as by the Emperor Hadrian during the Roman occupation of Britain. The question at the root of all of this is just how long can the social systems involved in the Palestinian conflict sustain their present policies until they come to the conclusion that they are unsustainable, failing and, ultimately, too cos tly. We might also recognize that there are unu sual precedents with regard to this vexed question of when do we reach the point of saying 'enough.' Evidently during the First World War there were those who took the view that, yes, there would be casualties, but if there were some of 'us' surviving when 'they' were all dead, then 'we' will have won. In the autumn of 2003 first pilots and then soldiers in Israel made it known that would refuse to fight in the war against the Palestinians.

In regard to the question of punishment in domestic systems, we are entitled to ask, 'how many prisons are to be built before the problem of crime is properly solved?' The obvious answer is that prisons can punish but they are not the means to solve problems. They are symptoms of the problem that has root causes. But authorities promise to incarcerate offenders and, if more prisons are required, then they will be built. There are even more social problems where authorities are either turning to t hreats and coercion – or are los ing control. Security guards patrol i n schools, in response to shootings and stabbings amongst pupil. Parents are increasingly frustrated in face of the problems presented to them by their defiant, unruly, disrespectful children and the number of one-parent families continues to increase.

Even the legal profession is dominated by an ethos of competition. Essentially one side wins and the other side loses. This is the way it is constructed, the outcome is either guilty or innocent, there is never a tie (though the Scottish legal system makes provision for the verdict of 'not proven'). This adversarial system has deep roots (see Langbein 2003). And it carries with it the risk that, in seeking a co nviction, evidence may be withheld, the credibility of witnesses demolished, scientific evidence poorly interpreted and innocent people imprisoned (in 2003 al one, in Great Britain, two women were acquitted on appeal and one found not guilty at trial in cases concerning the unexplained deaths of their infant children. It was assumed that these children were murdered; they were not, but died of Sudden Infant Death Syndrome, or 'cot deaths'). After many years in prison, six men convicted of setting off a bomb in Birmingham that killed many were set free; they had been wrongly convicted. So too were those convicted of setting off a bomb in Guildford, Surrey. The point of this series of comments about the legal system is that it is structured to get an outcome, not at so lving the problem. Moreover, justice is often mixed or confused with vengeance. Again this is rooted in an element of our J udaeo-Christian culture: an e ye for an eye and a tooth for a tooth. Except that an eye for an eye leaves us all blind in the long run.

In both of these sets of circumstances we might ask, where is all o f this leading us?

Might one likely outcome be the fractionation or atomization of societies, with individuation the preferred modus operandi for people and interactions with others, possible only indirectly, an exception rather than the norm? And then what, to the politics of an atomized Dystopia?

Second, where new norms of association are being developed, in sub-groups where there are different values in operation, not mainstream values, and/or where values of association and peaceful conflict resolution have been learned, then there might be scope to look at the effects of what we might call not the 'shower effect' but, on he contrary the 'bidet effect'. In other words, there may be changes at the lower reaches of the social pyramid, as opposed to the usual trend of ideas and innovations starting at the top and tricking down. We might cite here, for example, the developments of cooperatives amongst the poor, in advanced states, who come together to combine their resources and buy commodities in bulk, then consuming them from a central pool as required, as opposed to the quantities that supermarkets are willing to sell. We might also cite the example of credit unions formed by those 'outside' the usual channels of banking, who cooperate to fulfil their own felt needs. And, of course, we can turn to examples of neighbourhood schemes that are not only about economic cooperation, but also about sustaining their neighbourhood and their neighbours, improving their life-spaces and thus self-worth and self-dignity. Many of the colossal errors perpetrated in the high-period of post-war modernity resulted in new housing developments that gave rise to isolation, depression and the long-lamented 'loss of co mmunity'. This is not to lament a lost culture of poverty allied to neighbourlyness. On the contrary, it is to suggest that there is a widely shared view that community is a value worth preserving and, where it has been lost, it is worth re-creating.

In the light of the foregoing, it is clear th at we are in a period of deep confusion, politically, socially and otherwise. Some seek community, others seem to feel that isolation and creating a space-for-self is necessary.

How did we get here? At the level of international politics, we have been locked into a serie s of assumptions, not least that, in regard to the matter of security, there is only so much of it, s o that it is necessary for states, acting on behalf of its citizens (or in pursuit of the interests of its leaders), to seek more, at the expense of others. In other words, we have been locked into a politics of zero-sum: more for means less for them. This dynamic further picks up momentum in the pursuit of armaments, so that claims to more are backed up by the threat or use of force, whether this is in pursuit of land, resources or control of others, directly or indirectly. As a recent example, the Bush Administration has stated that American prosperity is not negotiable. For a domestic audience this is laudable and probably comforting. In the longer term, there will have to be negotiations about security and prosperity for Americans. The pursuit of economic growth comes with associated costs, whether or not it is th e relentless pursuit of oil (in the Middle East, the Caspian Basin or the Athabasca Tar Sands at the margin) or the pursuit of the American Dream, the latest manifestation of which is 'The Hummer.' This vehicle has a six-litre engine, weighs 3.9 tonnes and does 4.25 kilometers per litre of diesel fuel. More than 25,000 of these were sold in the first nine months of 2003 (The Australian, Dec 2 6 2003 p.10). On the crudest statistic – that the United States, with 4% of the world's population consumes 25% of the world's energy – we might simply ask not how long the US population can sustain this, but how long the rest of the planet will find this acceptable, es pecially since the gap between rich and poor is getting larger.

In summary, in international politics, we have lived with international norms of competition, which have, in turn, been consequential for the setting of foreign- and defence-policy goals. There are signs that this culture may be changing. From its inception in 1957 under the Treaty of Rome (and, before that, in its precursors, the European Coal and Steel Community and the European Atomic Energy Agency) the European Union has moved towards 'ever closer union' the guiding goal of the Rome Treaty itself. That goal is stated but there is no hint as to where the process could, or sh ould, finish. Integration is a p rocess and it remains controversial in many quarters. But we need to set the contemporary problems in a broad context. In 1870, 1914 and 1940, the French and the Germans were involved in violent wars that saw millions killed. So too were the British and most other European states involved. We are now in a situation where there are long-term and dependable expectations of peaceful change between amongst many states in Europe. It is not an exaggeration to say that conflict over money and agriculture represents a co nflict of a differen t order of magnitude as compared to what has gone before. There is much to learn here, especially in light not only of the birth of the modern international system in Europe but also in light of its violent past. Perhaps it is that nothing is given and nothing is immutable.

The international dimension is but one aspect of what amounts to a dominant culture of competition and conflict. In domestic systems, and in very recent decades, we have become slaves to notions such as 'look after number one,' 'nice guys finish last' and, most notably (from the renowned American football coach Vince Lombardy) 'winning is not the most important thing, it is th e only thing'. Arguably this has been serious in its implications for the way we behave in relation to each other. What, then, are th e prospects for the teams in every league and competition who are, ov erwhelmingly, the losers? How are t hey to cope, psychologically if nothing else? How have the values that underpin sport as healthy competition, worth in itself for the sake of taking part, rather than in the winning? Can this have anything to do with the spread of illegal drug use in sport, where athletes risk disgrace at best and death at worst in pursuit of 'victory'?

This code of competition has also gained momentum from the dominance of market economics in the last two decades, principally associated with the Reagan-Thatcher years, where there was a manifest switch to the political right. In this context, Thatcher asserted that ' there is no such thing as society.' Rather, she suggested, there were people and families, who were capable of knowing how to spend their own income. 'Keeping up with the Jones's' received a huge ideological boost and a clear justification. Twenty years later, the burden of consumer debt is colossal – and so is the burden of stress, in advanced societies.

Indeed, the Reagan-Thatcher years may have brought into sharp relief some of the essential foundations of economics as a social science. Schoolchildren and undergraduates alike learn the fundamental principles of scarcity and the rules of competition (perfect, imperfect, monopolistic and the like) in the very earliest stages of their encounter with the curriculum. Apart from processes of competition and allocation, there is a focus on wants (sometimes created by firms through advertising and other influences on consumers) and rather less on human needs. The contemporary dilemma in economics, local and global, is not a question of scarcity, for there are many sectors where there is massive excess capacity, stored agricultural surpluses and underused plant. The central problem is distribution, for there is food enough in the world to feed all, for example. Yet there is the problem of individuation and costs: why should I pay if nobody else will share costs with me? If nobody shares, it does not get done. Aid is, essentially a marginal concern in the running of economies, statistically and otherwise, for state authorities notionally are obliged to look after their own populations first.

We have said little of poorer societies, where the life chances of individuals are poor and, in many circumstances, deteriorating; since the end of the Cold War, the life-expectancy of the average Russian male has decreased markedly. In Africa, famine and AIDS combine (with corruption and violence) to catastrophic effect. And if these are the problems faced by peoples elsewhere, we should not be surprised that many (but not the vast majority) will seek to escape these conditions, if they have sufficient funds and are willing to engage with the risks of death, rape or discovery in order to be somewhere where they think they will be better off, perhaps seduced by television or internet images of a better life. There is nothing that is essentially new in this, for many poor people thought that the streets of London were paved with gold. What is unprecedented is the global reach and ambitions of those who seek to move somewhere else.

In relation to fears from abroad, the recent experience of otherness and difference is illuminating. 'Asylum seekers' and the like are a conspicuous problem for many. They are foreign and want to come 'here' from somewhere else. 'They' want 'our' jobs, it is said. 'They' will threaten 'our' culture it is assumed. Therefore they constitute a threat. Never mind that those states often striking these attitudes are nations of immigrants themselves, notably the United States and Australia but also, arguably, Britain. Often the response of the state authorities is resort to fast patrol boats, fences and added security checks at ports and airports. These are responses to the symptoms, not the causes. They are also easier responses, but the causes of the problems are systemic. Global capitalism promises much to many but does not deliver enough to enough. This we have learned, and so have the world's poor: and many of them resent it, resort to means to do something about it and often resort to violence. It is to state no more than the obvious, after fifty years of Peace Research, that the roots of violence and 'terror' are rooted in the conditions of poverty, isolation and lack of identity. Thus, a 'war on terror' is both the wrong metaphor, relying on the wrong means, if those means are military means. The problem is systemic in origin and systemic in terms of its solution, which does not mean a Mercedes or a 'Hummer' for all.

Whatever happened to the agenda of welfare economics? Or the agenda of debate associated with collective goods? Since we saw ourselves as a spinning ball in space, there has surely been an impetus to rethink the nature of our dominant ethic of competition and conflict, be it in parliaments, courts, markets, communities and global systems. We live in a finite space with finite resources (the debate about renewable fuels duly recognized). We h ave the metaphors of the global village and the world getting smaller. But we are b oth conservative in our beliefs and reluctant to shift to a d ifferent future which is unknowable and therefore threatening us with more insecurity. We find faith and succour, comfort and security in what we know, however faulty our knowledge. In an era of limits to growth and exploitation, we might investigate again the notion, explicated by Sherif almost forty years ago, of 'super-ordinate goals' which can be met through increased cooperation, with benefits for all, even those who think themselves to be rooted in deep conflict (Sherif 1967).

There may be a third issue of significance here too. Yes, states must confront the costs of doing what they do and, yes, they make be a forcing up of ideas 'from below'. There is a crisis of democracy. In the United States the pattern that is revealed over decades of recent presidential elections is that only 50% of those eligible to vote actually turn out to vote. This is the norm, not the exception. In Britain, too, there is a lo ss of faith in politics: many believe that they are not best served by politicians and political authorities. Interest in elections is falling and membership of political parties has fallen dramatically. Means of reviving interest in Britain have involved questions of electronic voting, voting in supermarkets and shopping centers and, most recently, lowering the voting age to s ixteen. In Australia. There us a debat e about the 'issue of faltering standards of truth and accountability in Australian public life generally' (Fitzgerald 2003 p.7).

But where there is a growth of political activity (and activism) is in the realm of single-issue politics. This includes questions of human rights, animal rights, globalization and its consequences, the environment, poverty, the ethics of global responsibility consequent upon globalization, feminism and women's rights to name but a few. In turn, these have led to the formation of organizations, small at first perhaps, but now politically significant, domestically and internationally. Amongst these we might number Greenpeace, Friends of th e Earth, Oxfam and Amnesty International. These are n ot states but they are actors in the global political system and they are actors by virtue of their ability to influence outcomes. It is significant that when the 'Rainbow Warrior,' the flagship of Greenpeace, got in the way of French nuclear testing in t he Pacific, the French blew it up in Auckland Harbour. Similarly, when the British government planned to sink a redundant oil platform in the north Atlantic, it was conspicuously prevented from doing so, again by Greenpeace, which filmed the episode and broadcast the event on television.

These and similar organizations represent a c hange in values in forty years and more. Oxfam began as a small shop run by volunteers in Oxford, as the Oxford Committee for Famine Relief. It n ow intervenes in areas of conflict and difficult where, often, state authorities are unwelcome and distrusted. It may be that this is but a manifestation of different values by an essentially 'comfortable' class within western democracies. But we should not merely dismiss it as such, or as an aspect of 'cash in the charity box' to assuage a guilty conscience. People pay money to join these organizations and they give much of their time to working on the agenda involved. In the wider public, symbolic events such as 'Live Aid' should not be dismissed as su perficial symbolism. American 'telethons' and other televised events raise millions every year for the poor an d under-privileged. The membership list of the Royal Society for the Protection of Birds comprise more than one million names, up from a total o f 60,000 les than forty years ago, more than the membership lists of the Labour, Conservative and Liberal Democrat parties combined. And all pay money to join it and by virtue of its size and voice it has some degree of influence over environmental and transport policy, especially as these are related to questions of conservation. Through and international partnership, Birdlife International, it h as part of a co llective and international voice. It may be said, by some, that this is a marginal issue on the political agenda,

But few political parties can afford to ignore it. T he 'Green Agenda' is a necessary part of the agenda of major political parties.

These may be ev idence of the articulation of alternative values that figure largely in the works of Fal k and Mendlovitz and their colleagues in the World Order Models Project, for they see a d ynamic where alternative values will materially affect the agenda of choice, as a prelude to institutional change. At the same time, these values and organization may be part of the emergent structure of what Chomsky calls 'the second superpower' at the start of the twenty-first century, namely world public opinion (Chomsky 2003). We might also recognize the extent to which, in 2003, the Iraq conflict brought increased demonstrations against the incursion into Iraq. Many took part in demonstrations for the first time in their lives. In a d iscussion of the contemporary American position as a p ax Americana, Kenneth Davidson observes that 'the Bush Administration overlooked two things: the foundation of A merican dominance is dollar hegemony – which their policies undermined – and the countervailing power of "legitimacy", based on the idea th at there are universal rules and values which are higher than the most powerful nation state and now instantly transmitted by a g lobalizes media' (Davidson 2003 p.5). This is a most interesting observation and is clearly inspired by Galbraith's notion of countervailing power in econ omic markets, where a counter to producer power emerges (see Galbraith 1954). This adds weight to Chomsky's notion of a second superpower.

Peace Research may, in Burton's terms, have made little impact on political thinking. But that is not the end of the story, for Burton goes on to say that 'the significance of these past several decades is not in practical progress towards the ultimate goal of peace. It is that there have been several important advances in thinking, which are now making possible communication with a wider audience, and helping to present an understandable and viable option to those who still fear change from the traditional deterrence frame. The task still lies ahead' (Burton 1996 p.3). The task of relating to state authorities and others should not be ruled out or thought impracticable, but it will take time: often authorities are the last to change as they are reluctant to embrace new realities. The Americans were, by way of example, convinced that they were winning and would win in Vietnam. Broadcasters were ahead of the authorities is saying that the war was unwinnable. The official agenda then changed dramatically.

Where there is, surely, great potential is in building bridges to these new actors in global politics, these International Non-governmental Organizations (INGOs), bringing together authoritative knowledge and creative insights and the new instrumentalities of world politics as represented by these INGOs. As it sought to establish itself, Peace Research engaged with the practical problem of instrumentalities, whether it b e the International Peace Research Association or otherwise. With, now, a degree of maturity, but still much to do, there is the possibility of engaging with existing actors, perhaps endowing them with more authority and/or legitimacy. This would be entirely consistent with the stated goal of Peace Research as having an ethic of being an applied science. If the research cancer specialist needs a h ospital to s ee his or h er work implemented, then the analogy with Peace Research and INGOs is one that is analogous and worthy of serious examination, not least in pursuit of synergies and increased effects. There still exists the task of engaging political authorities and other power-wielders. That task is still in urgent need of address.

In the longer term, and at a different level, there is the question of peace education, of which we already have made mention. But we need to add an other dimension here. In most countries, peace education is conspicuous by its absence. Where it is included in the curriculum, it is subsumed into wider discussions about civics or citizenship, or something similar. Progress may be seen to be made when it becomes an element of the curriculum in its o wn right. Taking children and students to a war memorial or a battle-site is important, but not enough. Seeing the 54,896 names on the Menin Gate, almost 60,000 at the Vietnam Memorial in Washington, D.C. and elsewhere clearly illustrates the impact of war; frequently, its pity and its futility, we argue. But the other part of the process is an engagement with the question of what to do next, in face of this suffering and loss. Peace is the presence of something as well as the absence of something else. Moreover, fifty years of Peace Research is there to be distilled into modules and courses that can be incorporated into school curricula, beyond, to repeat, religious understanding and civic education. The question of acculturation to peac e is also important, in face of the persistent controversies regarding the role of war toys in play, the viewing of violence on television and the competitive strategies fostered in the culture of computer games. Again, it is not simply the absence of 'Rambo' or 'Rocky' or 'The Exterminator'. It m ust be the presence of something positive, rather than the absence of the negative. There is a challenge to develop an agenda here, mindful of the notion that the proverbial 'good news newspaper' folds after a week and that, for news-editors, 'it it bleeds, it leads'.

This will not be easy. Firstly, because many will be suspicious of what they feel is tendentious and propagandistic. 'Twas ever thus. Secondly, however, where there an emphasis on education as equipping a s killed work-force to allow the country to compete in an era of globalization, with consequences in terms of what is deemed necessary as opposed to desirable, then the task becomes even more difficult. The implementation of the National Curriculum in Britain, for example, seems to have resulted in a hierarchy of subjects; the core and the marginal. Within three years, for example, students will be able to drop the study of a f oreign language ate the age of fourteen, after just three years of study.

International Relations, Strategic Studies and Peace Research

International relations is in serious trouble. The developments in strategic thinking are questionable at best and dangerous at worst, indeed jeopardizing global security even as the Cold War recedes into history. As Gunter Minnerup describes the situation 'The identification of the "West" with enlightened rationality and the "East" with atavistic unreason has become so ingrained that the very same people do not even realize it when, in a different context, they become the most ardent advocates of obs curantism themselves...The fact is that, at t he dawn of t he Twenty-first century, the Western world is in the grip of ideas so irrational that they would have seemed outlandish to the whirling dervishes of the Ottoman Empire' (Minnerup 2003 p.6).

International Relations started as In ternational Politics and some university departments and institutes adhere to the traditional rubric. But International Relations was meant to signify something wider and more encompassing, perhaps issues of economic security and increased numbers of international relationships that did not all involve states. But the foundational assumption was that the state-centric paradigm was at the core of the study. The process of adaptation, as the context within which the study of international relations takes place changes (see the earlier chapters in this book), has been a question of seeking to incorporate 'states plus', where the element of plus refers to the rise of multinational corporations, inter-governmental organizations (IGOS), international non-governmental actors (INGOs), other non-state actors (such as the Irish Republican Army, ETA, the Palestinian Liberation Organization, the Red Brigades, Frelimo, the African National Congress and the like). Only by bringing in these actors, with their capacity to influence outcomes, could appropriate explanations of international relations be engaged appropriately. These actors may not have had legal status, but they had a behavioural status; they existed and they made things happen. The British Government refused to deal with the IRA (because they were 'terrorists') and, indeed, at one point quite literally refused to let the voices of their spokesmen be heard, with actors speaking words over filmed interviews. But they were engaged, at first secretly and then overtly. Prison refused to silence them and overt violence against them radicalized more and led to a wave of recruitment.

International Political Economy emerged to encompass the politics of trade, industry and money. Both international politics and international economics allocate, but they allocate ac cording to diff erent logics. By the early seventies, international economics was too important to leave to the economists and relegated to the final chapters of the economics textbooks for the sake of completeness. Oil also became more overtly political with the price rises administered by the Organization of Petroleum Exporting Companies (OPEC) at the same time, a direct consequence of the Middle East war of 1973. Soon linkage politics was on the agenda, a product of developments in both the economic arena and arms control. Development, more specifically underdevelopment and debt questions relating to so-called Third World states were thrust onto the agenda, involving the World Bank, western banks and aid ag encies. Human Rights abuses became more conspicuous as the international system became more transparent and dissidents could find a v oice: the increased transparency might explain why it was that dissidents in the Soviet Union were incarcerated, whereas their predecessors had been 'liquidated'.

Borders of states became more porous. Interdependence appeared as a concept to try to explain this, later to give way to 'globalization'. Complexity was the order of the day and new conceptual schemes and approaches appeared to try to provide explanations of what was going on. A key distinction was drawn with regard to 'high' politics on the one hand (what states do, which was self-evidently important) and 'low' politics on the other, important, but not primary. At the boundaries of the discipline, some came close to th e boundary with Peace Research, now creating a grey area where the two met. Here we might include the works of R ob Walker, Ken Booth, Nicholas Wheeler and Tim Dunne, who have enhanced a rath er more humano-centric view of the agenda, perhaps even articulating further the agenda of global responsibility.

But, in its essential concerns, the discipline is still locked into an agenda dominated by the agenda of states, asserted to be the key actors in a system of self-help. Armed force, deterrence, diplomacy (see, for example, Berridge date), international law and foreign policy are still central concerns and still the stuff of textbooks, the sure indicator of what the subject is about. The curriculum has changed: Strategic Studies in the sixties gave way to International Security and, later, Global Security Issues and, then, Critical Security Studies. International Political Economy gave way to Politics of the World Economy. Innovations recognized the 'politicization' of areas thought previously to be be yond politics, such as th e International Politics of Sport (see Ho ulihan date), especially where states had sought to legitimize their claims to status by reference to medals won at major competitions. Human Rights became an explicit object of study, not merely an adjunct to law or ethics, but now a clearl y an international and political issue. So, too, with areas such as aerospace, tourism and transport. All claimed a place on the agenda of International Relations.

In other words, the discipline was dynamic and seeking to be relevant, but the various approaches that emerged to ex plain what was going on were locked into the existing paradigm of inter-state politics, albeit with a 'plus' element. The problem was that the paradigm was incapable of explaining what was going on. A focus on states is necessary, but not sufficient in terms of the dominant paradigm's capacity to ex plain global dy namics, of which states are bu t one part. The paradigm is partial and therefore problematic.

There was the breakdown of states that had been formed in the wake of the collapse of European empires. Thus we had the agenda of 'failed states' – or perhaps we should name them 'never-had a chance-states' for they lacked common values, common identities and fundamental legitimacy, their new flags, anthems and presidents notwithstanding. Internal conflicts soon followed, as in Nigeria, Indonesia (being comprised of thousands of islands that made up the Dutch East Indies, with almost no other common factor to unite its peoples), Sudan, Somalia, Cyprus and the rest. Principal amongst them might be numbered Iraq: it was formed to suit the requirements of the British and French state au thorities as th e Ottoman Empire was carved up after the First World War, with boundaries drawn on the map with little or no regard for the needs of Kurds, Sunnis or Shias amongst others. Thus, frequently, the sources of international conflict could only be explained in terms of the origins of domestic conflict, which was not, strictly, part of the remit of International Relations. Of course, the domestic sources of foreign policy were important (Rosenau 1968), but domestic conflict was a matter for other specialists.

Doubtless, this line of argument could be pursued. Yet we could ask a single, massive projective question; is any or all of this framework of thinking actually relevant to the processes of interaction that are the lives of the vast majority of people on the planet. Most of the decisions that affect them may be about day-to-day existence and survival: the availability of water, food and wood; the job in a low-wage plant controlled not by a local authority, but by a multinational corporation concerned with profit and loss as seen from London or New York. This is not simply about poorly paid in the Third World. Those in work in the developed West are now vulnerable to the logic of the balance sheets and the consequent shift to 'outsourcing', 'going offshore' and similar euphemisms, which means jobs are lost and are moved to areas of lower wage costs. The most recent phenomenon is the shift of call-centre jobs from Europe to India, where graduates are employed to handle inquiries about utilities in Britain and elsewhere. This is not to say that states are irrelevant: but are they primary influences in terms of decision-making for individuals, concerned with myriad other relationships.

Instead of looking at formal structures of states and government, where they are often the object of mistrust and suspicion, we ought to shift to a survey of behaviourially-grounded relationships: study not what people ought to do (and when they do not we cast them as deviants or lawbreakers) but what they do in the normal course of events.

International Relations studies structures and then processes between and amongst states and other actors. Peace Research has stimulated a shift towards a stress on relationships generally defined, of which interstate relations are but one part of a very complex whole, The key is to study the complexities of a global system that stresses the unity of the whole, as well as the relationships between the individual and the whole. Moreover, relationships that are not only conflictual and coercive, but also cooperative and legitimate.

Why should we move in this direction? As Burton stated thirty years ago, 'international politics has nothing to do with the real world; it is a game' (1974). By which he meant that it is a series of rules and norms that are questionable in relation to the realities of global politics. The relevance of the Burton comment springs to mind in looking at the State Visit of President Bush to Britain in the autumn of 2003. Not only did he need to be isolated from any encounters with ordinary Britons, but we witnessed the sight of Bush being driven from the rear of Buckingham Palace to be greeted, formally and with due pomp, by the Queen at the front door. Is this but one example of the games that states play?

In fact, as we have already suggested, states do nothing: people acting in the name of states assume roles and codes of conduct, to their own ends and purposes. Often, a Nelsonian blind eye is turned against repression and violence. In years gone by, in full knowledge of what was going on in Rumania, President Ceacescu was warmly welcomed to Britain. The excesses of the former dictator of Uganda, Idi Amin, were well-known, but the rules of international conduct prevented intervention, until Amin intervened unlawfully in the affairs of an adjacent state, at which point external forces intervened to ov erthrow him. Nelson Mandela was branded a terrorist, and the ANC with him. Then he became a respected President following his release from Robben Island and his assumption of the presidency of South Africa. In light of these and similar circumstances, we can be sympathetic to then view that diplomacy requires both a long memory and the ability to forget as circumstances require. Can it be the case, still, that states have no perpetual friends and no perpetual enemies, but only perpetual interests? What of the needs of citizens and subjects?

Furthermore, we should beware of what we have called the statist pretence. That is, the presumption that we have somehow reached the ultimate level of sophistication and maturity in terms of our political organization because we are organized into state, which we have invented and tried to legitimate. What are the grounds for assuming that the state is the be-all and end-all of political organization? It will do only insofar as it is f unctional, which means serving functions above and beyond its own survival, often uniting populations on specious grounds and calls to un ite in face of a perceiv ed (or con structed) insecurity. In certain states the imperative is to split and shift to legitimate levels of participation, where people have a say, as opposed to being told. In certain circumstances there may be demands an need to shift to a level of authority above and beyond the state. There may still be a legitimate role for it to play. But to turn against an agenda of future adaptation and fail to encompass the future in any meaningful debate about where we go forward from here, with a process of change and adaptation central to this (with the consent of the people) is f acile and dangerous, perhaps tempting authorities into further measures of repression and control.

If this a d im view of International Relations, then the agenda of Strategic Studies is hardly more propitious. We might have found comfort in the demise of the Cold War (in the course of which something of the order of 50,000 nuclear weapons were deployed; we may feel that we have an obligation to explain to future generations why this was deemed necessary as a means to security). A decade and more on there are serio us concerns about the militarization of space, the dash for which has seen the United States consigning the 1972 Anti-Ballistic Missile Treaty to the rubbish bin of Cold war detritus, with the rationale that it was a product of the Cold War, the Cold War is over, therefore the treaty has no enduring validity. The prospects for a universal test ban on nuclear weapons are remote. Much has been said about the problems of chemical and biological weapons but here to there is no universal prohibition in prospect.

A Rand Corporation report, dated May 2003, con cluded that 'the potential for an accidental or u nauthorized nuclear missile launch in Russia or th e United States has\grown over the past decade despite warmer US-Russian relation' (quoted by Chomsky 2003 p.221). The increased need, apparently, for missiles to be launched on warning, with the minimal scope for human agency, is an especial cause of concern. Moreover, 'traditional policy has been turned upside down' as nuclear weapons have become 'a tool of war-fighting rather than deterrence' (Ivo

Daalder, quoted by Chomsky 2003 p.2 22). In which case the Nuclear Use Theorists off the 1970s were just the pioneers in the field of this bizarre approach to security.

Is this salient, but essentially anachronistic, in terms of long-term survival of the human race on this planet? Are there not good grounds for assuming that Peace Research constitutes a partial promise, at leas t, of long-term peace an d security based on human interactions at all social levels that is based on legitimate relationships that are devoted to fulfilling human need rather than the interests of states and their leaders; and where problems are resolved rather than coerced; and where people are th e primary level of analysis in all of ou r studies? Systems, societies, states and collectivities are but means to an end.

There is ev idence that the shift out of one paradigm and into another is underway. We have already identified other actors and forces in global politics. Also, we have observed that not only are state boundaries porous, but that relationships span boundaries of states, regardless of the legal existence of such frontiers. More than thirty years ago, Burton posited the existence of a World Society, constructed of a myriad of behavioural relations and interacting systems, long before the emergence of the notion of globalization. The key to the new paradigm is a focus on relationships.

The key to an ontology of peace is rooted in the notion not of 'peace' based on threats, coercion and control, but on adaptation, conflict resolution and change, with legitimacy a key component in all of this. An ontology of peace is a di fferent assumption about what is real and what is illusory. It changes priorities.

Traditionally, peace has been thought to be rather limited in its meanings. In International Relations, peace has meant the absence of general war. NATO, it was said, was vital element of 'keeping the peace in Europe' for forty years. But Europe was a most heavily armed continent, crises were frequent, domestic conflicts were common (in Spain, Ireland, Italy, France, Belgium and elsewhere) and dissent was vocal. Similarly, the period 1815 to 1914 was termed the century of peace since there were no general wars involving the Great Powers. But what of the American Civil War (hardly incidental in terms of the evolution of total war), the Austro-Prussian War, t he Franco-Prussian war and the Scramble for Africa? The fact is that the traditional notions of peace hide periods of widespread violent conflict and repression. Good order in the colonies, keeping the indigenous populations stable, was base on coercion and repression. George Orwell's record of his time in the Burma police force might be a good place to begin to un derstand these processes, not based in the nineteenth century, but the middle years of the twentieth. All of this was sustained by a culture of dominance, expressed in the periodicals of the day and in the literature that was presented to the mass publics as literacy spread. Battle honours of regiments and the regimental flags were hung in churches and Cathedrals as sacrifice was honoured and du ty to th e Empire recognized. They are th ere still, in stone, for all to see. More recently, the thousands of Americans who were killed in Vietnam are re membered in Washington, D.C. an at ce meteries across the United States; the millions of Vietnamese who died are honoured nowhere.

Short of overt violence, as Galtung has indicated, many live in pitiful, squalid conditions of little hope and much despair. To come to the point, the reason that there is so much violence in the world is because there is not enough peace. Peace is the presence of positive qualities, not merely the absence of negative ones. Not least of these is that people be regarded as human beings, just like us. Some of the research that came out of the Cold war focused on the images of the enemy (see Kelman 1965). Americans who did meet Russians, ordinary people, came out of the confrontation saying, in effect, they are just like us! What, we might wonder, did they expect to find? Green people with three heads? When Burton brought together individuals in conflict in the earliest days at the Centre for the Analysis of Conflict, after three days (and previously steeped in conflict) both parties saw that they wanted precisely the same as each other, and they escaped from te zer-sum approach.

In terms of images of the other, there is much to learn from. Dower has shown us how the Japanese were de-humanized by the American media – and popular opinion – during the war the Pacific. In Korea, the enemy was reduced to 'gooks'. Likewise, in Vietnam. Perhaps this is necessary to train men and women to fight and kill as required under orders; maybe it is easier to kill a th ing as opposed to a person. But studies of post-war effects are now much better known than they once were. In the First World War, the effects of 'shell-shock' were denied; there were only malingerers and deserters. Now, soldiers are kn own to suffer from post-traumatic stress disorder and are t reated accordingly. To take orders and to h ell with the consequences is deemed rather passé these days, presenting many new problems for the post-modern military. But there are wider implications not simpy in terms of the way the enemy is labeled, but also the lexicon of conflict. It is in creasingly detached and 'sanitized'. 'Think of the term heard so often recently: *collateral damage.* The mark of t his discourse is to use what I call th e "numbing phrase," which deceives not by outright negation of reality (though it may be accompanied by overt lies) but by spraying a verbal mist that anesthetizes so that the pain of human suffering and devastation cannot be felt or even recognized. In contrast "the apt phrase" enables clear reco gnition, stimulates the ethical imagination and impedes the evasion of truthfulness' (Lacey 2003 p.21).

So how do we engage with 'otherness' if we only encounter 'otherness' via television, through folk knowledge ('we Protestants in Belfast know what the Catholics are like, because we have been told; it is obvious. So we do not want to meet them, besides they live apart from us, beyond a wall or a boun dary'), stereotypes and absorbing the lessons of history. This is an important issue on the agenda, not least because so many people s eem to perform phenomenal mental acrobatics in order to maintain cognitive consistency. They may like an individual from another race or country, because they know him or her from their workplace or elsewhere; but they dislike the 'rest of them' for unspecified and probably un-specifiable reasons. There is a poten tially significant conjunction here between Peace Research on the one hand and Cultural and Media Studies on the other. We know full well that state authorities who commit forces to armed conflict are sensitive about the casualty rate. But they are also sensitive to images of death and suffering. The Vietnam War changed the agenda radically: it i s well-nigh impossible nowadays to consider that authorities would permit the showing of images of, say, a monk setting fire to himself, a prisoner being shot dead in front of a camera, a soldier setting fire to a village ('in order to save it) or a child covered in burns inflicted by napalm. All of these –and more – were transmitted during Vietnam. Few images of a similar nature came out of t he Falklands/Malvinas conflict, the First Gulf War or the most recent. Or, for that matter, East Timor, Tienanmen Square, Bosnia and Rwanda.

It is also worth remembering that the attacks on New York and Washington, D.C. and the crash of an aircraft in Pennsylvania, saw something of the order of 3,000 people killed. More than twice that number were killed in Srebrenica. One was a highly visible, and consequently shocking, set of images. The other was largely invisible, but no less shocking. Insofar as ecological protestors suggest that we, as consumers, should pay the full costs of what we do (rather than merely the going economic rate) then perhaps, as citizens – and responsible ones at that – we should be prepared to pay the full political, economic and emotional costs of conflict. Currently, our collective comfort comes at a p rice we do n ot often acknowledge, if we acknowledge it at all. Presumably, authorities know that this is a sensitive issue, above all others. In the Iraq conflict of 2003 we saw, for the first time, correspondents 'embedded' with army units. Certainly a novelty, but it is tempting to come to the conclusion that the length of news coverage was in inverse proportion to the news content. As the Chinese philosopher Lao Tsu wrote two centuries ago 'fail to honour people and they will fail to honour you'. Are the 'wages of spin' skepticism, disbelief, cynicism and, ultimately, a crisis o f democracy. Or, for a different example, simply recall the look on Ceasescu's face when the assembled Bucharest crowd said 'No'!

In other words. confronting the realities, a nd costs, of a war, violence and conflict culture might be a significant step along the way to not only a politics of peace but also a culture of peace.

What might this look like? So-called 'Realists' and cynics are clear as to how they view these things. As Time magazine reported 'It may be that idealism needs naivete to survive' (Time December 29 2003 p.30).

So, there we have it. In these terms, a peaceful society is pie in the sky. If it does happen, maybe it will be just a bunch of touchy-feely types who hug trees and talk to birds. We do not have to follow this line of reasoning any further. In summary, it just will not happen, because it is illusory, naïve and all the rest.

On the other hand, to be idealist is to be a realist and a courageous one at that. The pioneers – B urton, Kenneth and Elise Boulding, Galtung, Singer – showed both courage, audacity, 'nerve' and resilience as they set out to go beyond the mainstream. They were not prisoners of the dominant assumptions about what was and was not 'real'. They were idealist in their assumptions and realistic in their programmes. There is a painting in the National Gallery of Australia in Canberra by Bea Maddock, with the title 'we live in the meanings we are able to discern.' We would do well to try to understand what that means and what is implied by it.

A peaceful society is not a society devoid of conflict. It is a society where conflict exists (and students of conflict have discovered that conflict is functional in many circumstances) but where it is approached differently and resolved, not merely suppressed or settled, soon to re-emerge. It is also a society where change and adaptation are addressed as norms; anticipated, planned for and adjusted to. It is a society where the fundamental principle of systems and relationships is that they are consensual and legitimate, where differences are tolerated, encouraged and fostered. It is a society where there are no 'deviants', but where there may be some who are ill and in need of medical treatment, as opposed to marginalization. Above all, it is dedicated to the fulfillment of human needs, the cause of human betterment and the eradication of structural violence. Moreover, Peace Research has demonstrated that knowledge about these features of a peaceful society is existing or within our grasp. It has been discovered, explained and recorded.

Finally, perhaps the primary effect of Peace Research has been to demonstrate the profound limitations of a concept at the root of so much of our traditional knowledge. Namely, the concept of 'human nature'. In stressing human needs and human relationships, peace researchers have discovered societies that are not competitive, inherently violent and so on. In explaining the origins of behaviour in terms of 'nurture' rather than in terms of the overwhelmingly dominant issue of 'nature', we may have found the means to escape the pressures of an overbearing culture, where there is a clash between 'good and evil', where murderers are 'the embodiment of evil' (as opposed to products of abuse and dysfunctional processes of socialization in families and schools) and there is an obligation to conform.

Maybe Nisbet got it right in suggesting that the biggest problem is the question of culture and 'civilization', especially a culture of violence. And, we might add, a culture of punishment, which may be another way of saying doing violence. If Peace Research has shown an alternative to that culture, then its achievement is immense. But there is still more to do. And there are more people doing it than ever before.

And, finally, all is mutable. Once upon a time, we assumed that the Earth was the centre of the Universe; that the Earth was flat; that witches and heretics were to be burned; that children should be sent down mines and up chimneys; that women were to be subservient; that children were to be seen and not heard; that slavery was part of the natural order of things; and that patients with an illness should be 'bled'. We can change, but find some habits of thought almost super-resistant to change. We look around, bemused and come to the conclusion that we struggle to do our best, but convinced that there is no alternative, other than to try harder with the devices we had. In looking back on changes that were effected, we find comfort in the view that our times are, somehow, more difficult than theirs.

But what, some may ask, are the alternatives? Consider the comment of Arthur Waskow, in regard to the question of prison and punishment; 'the only full alternative is building the kind of society that does not need prisons. A decent redistribution of power and income, so as to put out the hidden fire of burning envy that now flares up in crimes of property…and a decent state of community that can support, reinvigorate and truly rehabilitate those who suddenly become filled with fury or despair and can face them not as "objects" – criminals – but as people who have committed illegal acts, as have almost all of us' (Quoted in Davis 2003 p.105).

We have progressed in these and other realms. We h ave failed to make progress in matters of war and peace since, with few exceptions, we thought that they were part of the natural order of things. We did our best to avoid wars, but eradication was thought impossible. What are the alternatives? War, as Margaret Mead told us decades ago, is an invention. It is not part of the 'natural order of things'. That being the case, we have it in our hands to change the agenda of choice. Peace Research has shown what kinds of choices, means and goals are available to us – and what the consequences and costs of sticking to our current habits and practices are.

As Michael Banks has put it, the most important revolutions are revolutions in ideas. And the American physicist Lee Smolin has argued 'we are abandoning the idea that the organization or beauty of any system, whether it be biological, ecological, economic or cosmological, is imposed from the outside, in favour of the conception that they arise internally by natural processes of self-organization. This is why Darwin is so important...I believe that we are s eeing the gradual incorporation of this insight into all the sciences that study the organization of systems, from cosmology to fundamental physics to the organization of human societies. This leads to t he replacement of explanations in terms of abs olute principles which are held to be eternally true with explanations that are historical and recognize the tremendous variety of possible outcomes of processes like natural selection' (Smolin, 1999 p.134).

These processes continue, and Peace Research evolves to be both means and mirror. But, there is a 'but;' 'One of the conditions for bringing about fundamental social change is bold, committed action, which stakes itself without the certitude of success...Ethically intelligent action cannot be carried out with certitude of being successful, for whether or not valued possibilities are realizable depends (causally), in part, on the committed actions of those who value them' (Lacey 2003 p.21). There, in short, is the impulse to Peace Research and., still, in troubled times, its guiding ethos.

The last word is from neither Peace Research, nor from a formal philosopher, but it carries sufficient weight for the task, and more. 'The ultimate human mystery may not be anything more than the claims on us of clan and race, which may yet turn out to have the power, because they defy the rational mind, to kill the world' (Arthur Miller quoted in Rushdie 2002 p.51).

Bibliography

Adam, B. (1995), *Timewatch*, Oxford, Polity Press.

Anderson, P. (1992), *English Questions*, London, Verso.

Biskind, P. (1983), *Seeing is Believing*, London, Pluto Press.

Bond, M. (2003), 'The Pursuit of Happiness', *New Scientist*, 10 October.

Booth, K. (1997)' 'Security and Self: Confessions of a fallen realist', in K. Krause and M. Williams (eds), *Critical Security Studies*, London, UCL Press.

Boulding, E. (1988), *Building a Global Civic Culture*, Syracuse, Syracuse University Press.

Boulding, E. and K.E. Boulding (1995), *The Future*, London, Sage Publications.

Boulding, K.E. (1968), *Beyond Economics: Essays on society, religion and ethics*, Ann Arbor, University of Michigan Press.

Boulding, K.E. (1978), *Stable Peace*, Austin, University of Texas Press.

Bronowski, J. (1978), *The Origins of Knowledge and Imagination*, New Haven and London, Yale University Press.

Buchan, A. (1974), *Can International Relations be Professed?*, Oxford, Oxford University Press.

Bull, H. (1977), *The Anarchical Society*, London, Macmillan.

Bullock, A. and O. Stallybrass (eds) (1977), *The Fontana Dictionary of Modern Thought*, London, Fontana Books.

Burleigh, M. (2001), *The Third Reich: A new history*, London, Pan Books.

Burton, J.W. (1962), *Peace Theory*, New York, Alfred Knopf.

Burton, J.W. (1964), 'Peace Research and International Relations', in *Journal of Conflict Resolution*, Vol. 3, pp. 281–286.

Burton, J.W. (1965), *International Relations: A general theory*, Cambridge Cambridge University Press.

Burton, J.W. (1969), *Conflict and Communication*, London, Macmillan.

Burton, J.W. and F.S. Northedge, 'Interstate or World Society?', Open University Broadcast.

Burton, J.W. (1990), *Conflict: Resolution and Prevention*, Basingstoke, Macmillan.

Burton, J.W. (1996), 'Creating Nonviolent Futures', Plenary Address to the IPRA Conference, Brisbane, Australia.

Caute, D. (1978), *The Great Fear*, London, Simon & Schuster.

Chatfield, C. (1979), 'International Peace Research: The field defined by dissemination', in *Journal of Peace Research* xvi.2.

Chomsky, N. (2003), *Hegemony or Survival Crows Nest*, NSW, Allen and Unwin.

Clark, M.E. (2002), *In Search of Human Nature*, London, Routledge.

Clark, R. (1978), *Bertrand Russell*, Harmondsworth, Pelican Books.

Cochran, M (1999), *Normative Theory in International Relations: A pragmatic approach*, Cambridge, Cambridge University Press.

Crane, D. (1972), *Invisible Colleges: Diffusion of knowledge in scientific communities*, Chicago and London, University of Chicago Press.

Curle, A. (1971), *Making Peace*, London, Tavistock Publications.

Davis, A. (2003), *Are Prisons Obsolete?*, London, Seven Stories Press.

De Reuck, A.V.S and J. Knight (eds), *Conflict in Society*, London, Churchill.

Deutsch, K.W. (1965), 'Preface to the Second Edition', in Wright, Q., *A Study of War* (second edition), Chicago, University of Chicago Press.

Dukes, F.M. (1996), *Resolving Public Conflict*, Manchester, Manchester University Press.

Dunn, D.J. (1995), ' International Relations and the Neglect of Culture', Staffordshire papers in International Relations Stoke on Trent (May).

Dunn, D.J. (2004), *From Power Politics to Conflict Resolution*, Basingstoke, Palgrave.

Edmead, F. (1971), *Analysis and Prediction in International Mediation*, New York, UNITAR.

Ellison, R. (1952), *Invisible Man*, London Gollancz.

Fisher, R. (1997), *Interactive Conflict Resolution*, Syracuse, Syracuse University Press.

Fitzgerald, M. (2003), 'The Enemy', in *The London Review of Books*, 18 December, pp. 8–10.

Freedman, L. (1986), 'The Crisis in Nuclear Strategy', in P. Paret (ed.), *Makers of Modern Strategy: From Macchiavelli to the nuclear age*, Princeton, Princeton University Press.

Galbraith, J.K. (1958), *The Affluent Society*, Harmondsworth, Pelican Books.

Galtung, J. (1964), 'Editorial', in *Journal of Peace Research*, 1(1).

Galtung, J. (1970), 'Why a Bulletin of P eace Proposals?', in *Bulletin of Peace Proposals*, 1(1).

Galtung, J. (1975), 'Peace: Research, education and action', *Essays in Peace Research*, Volume 1 Oslo, Eijlers.

Griffiths, M. a nd D. O'Callaghan (2001), *International Relations: The key concepts*, London, Routledge.

Hamilton, C. (2003), *Growth Fetish Crows Nest*, NSW, Allen and Unwin.

Haskell, T.S. (1977), *The Emergence of Professional Social Science*, Urbana and London, University of Illinois Press.

Hickie, J. and R.S.P. Elliot, *Ulster: A case study in conflict theory*, London, Longman.

Hobsbawm, E. (2002), 'War and Peace', *The Guardian*, 23 February.

Hobsbawm, E. an d R. Ranger (1983), *The Invention of Tradition*, Cambridge, Cambridge University Press.

Hoffmann, M. (1987), ' Critical Theory and the Inter-paradigm Debate', in *Millennium: The Journal of International Studies* 16, pp. 231–249.

Hofstadter, R. (1963), *Anti-intellectualism in American Life*, New York, Alfred Knopf.

House of Representatives (1978), National Academy of Peace and Conflict Resolution: Hearings before the Sub-committee on International Operations of the Committee on International Relations, 95th Congress, Second Session January 24 and 25. USGPO.

Hubbard, G. (1974), *Quaker by Convincement*, Harmondsworth, Pelican Books.

Hughes, R. (1993), *The Culture of Complaint*, Oxford, Oxford University Press.

Hveem, H. (1973), *Peace Research: Historical development and future prospects*, Proceedings of the Fourth IPRA Conference, pp. 198–208.

Hynes, S. (1992), *A War Imagined*, London, Pimlico Books.

Kaye, E. (ed.) (1987), *Peace Studies: The hard questions*, London, Rex Collings.

Kelman, H.C. (ed.) (1965), *International Behavior*, New York, Holt, Rinehart and Winston.

Kelman, H.C. (1968), *A Time to Speak*, San Francisco, Jossey Bass.

Kelman, H.C. (1984), 'Foreword', in M.H. Banks (ed.), *Conflict in World Society*, Brighton, Wheatsheaf Books.

Kenniston, K. (1971), *Youth and Dissent: The rise of a new opposition*, New York, Harcourt, Brace and Yovanovich.

Kerman, C. (1974), *Creative Tension*, Ann Arbor, The University of Michigan Press.

Kuhn, T.S. (1962), *The Structure of Scientific Revolutions*, Chicago, University of Chicago Press.

Kruzel, J. and J.N. Rosenau (1989), *Journeys through World Politics*, Lexington and Toronto, D.C. Heath.

Lawler, P. (1 995), *A Question of Values: Johan Galtung's Peace Research*, Boulder, Colorado, Lynne Reinner.

Lenz, T. (1955), *Towards a Science of Peace*, New York, Bookman Associates.

Mack, A. (1985), *Peace Research in the 1980s*, Canberra, Australian National University.

Mackenzie, W.J.M. (1967), *Politics and Social Science*, Harmondsworth, Pelican Books.

Manuel, F.E. and F.P. Manuel (1979), *Utopian Thought in the Western World*, Oxford, Basil Blackwell.

McRobbie, A. (2005), *The Uses of Cultural Studies*, London, Sage Publications.

McSweeney, B. (199 9), *Security, Identity and Interests: A Sociology of International Relations*, Cambridge, Cambridge University Press.

Medwar, P.B. (1986), *Evening Standard*, 2 April.

Melko, M. (19 73), *52 Peaceful Societies*, Oakville, Ontario Canadian Peace Research Institute.

Miall, H. *et al.* (1999), *Contemporary Conflict Resolution*, Oxford, Polity Press.

Mitchell. C.R and M.H. Banks (1996), *Handbook of Conflict Resolution*, London, Pinter.

Morgenthau, H.J. (1949), *Politics Among Nations*, New York, Alfred Knopf.

Myrdal, G. (no date), *Peace Research and the Peace Movement*.

Nathan, O. and H. Norden (1960), *Einstein on Peace*, New York, Schocken Books.

Nisbet, R. (1976), *The Social Philosophers*, London, Paladin Books

Noel-Baker, P. (1958), *The Arms Race*, London, John Calder.

Nye, J.S. (2002), *The Paradox of American Power*, Oxford, Oxford University Press.

Olsen, O.J. and I.M. Jarvad, 'The VietNam Conference papers: A case study in the failure of Peace Research', in *Peace Research Society* (International) Papers Vol. xiv.

Pardeesi, G. (ed.) (1982), *Contemporary Peace Research*, Atlantic Highlands, New Jersey Humanities Press.

Pruitt, D.G. and R. Snyder (eds), *Theory and Research on the Causes of War*, Englewood Cliffs, N.J., Prentice Hall.

Rabinow, P. (1984), *The Foucault Reader*, Harmondsworth, Pelican Books.

Ramsbotham, D. (2003), *Prisongate: The shocking state of Britain's prisons and the need for visionary change*, London, Free Press.

Reid, H.S and E.J. Yanarella (1976), 'Toward a Critical Theory of Peace Research in the United States: The Search for an "intelligible core"', in the *Journal of Peace Research*, 13(4), pp. 315–341.

Rosenau, J.N. (1968), *Domestic Politics and Foreign Policy*, New York, Free Press.

Rotblat, J. (1972), *Scientists in the Quest for Peace*, Cambridge, The MIT Press.

Rushdie, S. (2002), *Step Across This Line: Collected non-fiction 1992–2002*, London, Jonathan Cape.

Russett, B.M. and M. Kramer (1973), 'New Editors for an Old Journal', in *Journal of Conflict Resolution*, 17(1).

Sandole, D.J.D. and H. van der Werwe (1993), *Conflict Resolution: Theory and practice*, Manchester, Manchester University Press.

Parsons, T. (1951), *The Social System*, New York, Free Press.

Schmid, H. (1968), 'Politics and Peace Research', in *Journal of Peace Research*, 3, pp. 217–232.

Senghaas, D. (19 73), 'Peace Research in the Federal R epublic of Germany', in *Journal of Peace Research*, 10(3).

Shaw, M. (1991), *Post-military Society*, Cambridge, Polity Press.

Shepard, C. *et al.* (1993), *Peace and War: Discovering the past*, Y9, London, John Murray.

Sherif, M. (1967), *Group Conflict and Cooperation*, London, Routledge and Kegan Paul.

Singer, J.D. (1965), *Human Behaviour and International Politics*, Chicago, Rand McNally.

Singer, J.D. (1968), *Quantitative International Politics*, New York, Free Press.

Singer, J.D. (1976a), 'An Assessment of Peace Research', in *International Security*, Summer, pp. 118–137.

Singer J.D. (1976b), 'Preface', in J. Dedring, *Recent Advances in Peace and Conflict Research*, Beverley Hills and London, Sage Publications.

Smoke, R. (1975), 'National Security Affairs', in F.I. Greenstein and N.W. Polsby (eds), *Handbook of Political Science*, Vol. 8, International Politics Reading, Mass. Addison Wesley.

Southwood, P. (1991), *Disarming Military Industries*, Basingstoke, Macmillan.

Terriff, T. *et al.* (1999), *Security Studies Today*, Cambridge, Polity Press.

Thee, M. (1970), 'Prefatory Note', in *Bulletin of Peace Proposals*, 1(1), p. 3.

Thompson, E.P. (1968), *The Making of the English Working Class*, London Gollancz.

Tidwell, A.C. (1998), *Conflict Resolved? A Critical Assessment of Conflict Resolution*, London, Pinter.

UNESCO (2000), *World Directory of Peace Research and Training Institutions* (9th edition) Paris.

Vasquez, J. *et al.* (1995), *Beyond Confrontation: Learning conflict resolution in the post Cold War era*, Manchester, Manchester University Press.

Walker, R.B.J. (ed.) (1984), *Culture, Ideology and World Order*, Boulder, Westview.

Wallace, M. (1972), 'The Radical Critique of Peace Research: An exposition and interpretation', in *Peace Research Reviews* iv(4).

Wallerstein, I. (1974), *The Modern World System*, New York, Academic Press.

Wallerstein, I. (1979), *The Capitalist World Economy*, Cambridge, Cambridge University Press.

Wehr, P. and M. Washburn (1976), *Peace and World Order Systems*, London, Sage.

Wright, Q. (1955), *The Study of International Relations*, Chicago, University of Chicago Press.

Wright, Q. (1965), *A Study of War* (2nd edition) Chicago, University of Chicago Press.

Index